Growing Together in Christ:
Personal development in the religious life

Growing Together in Christ:

Personal development in the religious life

edited by
Jonathan Cotton OSB

New City
London   Dublin   Edinburgh

Based on an original edition in Italian
Crescere insieme in Cristo
published by Città Nuova, Rome, 1988
First published in Great Britain 1991
by New City
57 Twyford Avenue, London W3 9PZ
© New City – London 1991

British Library Cataloguing in Publication Data
Growing Together in Christ: personal development in the
religious life.
1. Christian life
I. Cotton, Jonathan II. Crescere insieme in Cristo. *English*
248.4

ISBN 0–904287–32–7

Typeset in Great Britain by
Chippendale Type Ltd., Otley, West Yorkshire
Printed and bound in Great Britain by
Billing and Sons Ltd., Worcester

Fr Joseph Savastano

DEDICATION

These essays are dedicated to a Pallotine, Fr Joseph Savastano, who is well-known in his own order, but of course is relatively unknown to the majority of our readers. This book is dedicated to him because he was a living example of all it is trying to convey. The reason is that he was deeply imbued with the life and spirit of his own order – so much so that he was given the task of re-defining the aims, objectives and spirit of the Pallotines in the post Vatican II Church, a labour that took seventeen years. At the same time, he was immersed in the spirituality of unity of the Focolare Movement, a spirituality that enabled him to rediscover the gift of his own founder.

Fr Joseph died on 23 January 1988, with his life's work and his own personal journey in the spiritual life complete. In all he did he exemplified the nickname he had been given in the Focolare Movement of Micor, from misericordia *meaning mercy and loving-kindness. Fr Angelo Beghetto OFM Conv., who knew him well and shared with him in living the spirituality of unity, wrote of Fr Joseph after he died; what follows is taken largely from what he wrote.*

Micor was born at Fontanafredda in Rocca Monfina, Caserta, Italy, on 26 February 1916. At the age of 18 he consecrated his life to God in the society for the Catholic Apostolate, founded by St Vincent Pallotti in 1835. He was ordained priest at the age of 23. When he was asked about his calling from God, he used to say that all his life he had intended to enter a religious order.

In 1949 he was elected Provincial of the Italian Province. Later he became a parish priest. It was in 1950 that he got to know the Focolare Movement and its life of unity, and he felt an immediate attraction to it.

His compassion knew no bounds. Whatever the hour and whoever came to him, it expressed itself naturally, simply and with a consummate tact. It was a reflection of the great love he felt, and fostered, for Mary, the Mother of Mercy, and many people came to know God's love through him and were converted.

He became Vicar General and Consultor of the Pallotine Society, remaining so to the end of his life. He had a profound understanding of Pallotti's charism and he embodied it in the new Constitutions he drew up, called the 'Fundamental Law', upon which he worked for seventeen years, right to his last days, rendering an invaluable service to his order and to the Church.

In February 1986 he was taken seriously ill. The doctors operated, but they held out no hope of a cure. Micor was fully aware of this, but he continued on his way, going peacefully towards his meeting with the Lord. He remained always faithful and vigilant, although he began to find his strength was flagging. During this time he stayed very close to his friends.

Then, having learnt how ill he was, Chiara Lubich, the foundress of the Focolare Movement, came to visit him. It was November 1987. Only at that point did she find out about all the work he was doing for his order. What struck her particularly, as she said, was that in him you could see 'a true member of his own order, a true priest, a true "child of the kingdom of heaven".'

The very next day Micor wrote to her: 'Your coming here and your invitation to me to explain my life and work to you have meant a rebirth for me, making more clear one aspect of unity: what is yours is mine and what is mine is yours . . . It's true, the name you gave me [Micor] is really beautiful. I'm often deeply moved by it. It engrafts me always more deeply into St Vincent.' Then, after a page of writing, he ended by saying, 'Paradise is filled with Mary's merciful prayer. I will sing of the mercies of the Lord for all eternity. I will sing of Mary's mercies for all eternity.'

Throughout his illness, he remained in close contact with the Focolare Centre for Religious, which is a small group of religious who have been given permission by their Superiors to work for all the religious who are in touch with the Focolare. He was always an example, a stimulus and a support to them, and those of his friends who were with him at every stage of his life as a religious in contact with the Focolare, united with him in that love which is God, saw how his wisdom, love and compassion were perfected as he slowly wasted away.

Then on 10 December 1987 he was admitted to hospital. His room soon became like a shrine visited by all sorts of people, and his bed became like an altar on which he celebrated the Mass of his own suffering, offering his sacrifice with joy. Indeed, when

Chiara visited him in the following January, as the members of the Focolare were trying to live the 'Word of Life' Perfect love casts out fear (following the Focolare practice of focussing each month on a Word of the Gospel), she was struck by how apt it was. He was the embodiment of this Word. Others said the same. 'If someone has true love, they are like a child in the arms of its father. They no longer fear anything – other people, events, life or death. They simply trust and are at peace.'

In the end, Micor said his final 'Yes, here I am' of complete abandonment to God. He asked both his Father General and Chiara to offer him to the Lord 'for the good of everyone', and he added that he was in the fullness of joy simply because 'it's nothing to do with me. I believe that it's because I have responded to God's call through Mary.'

At the funeral Fr Victor Vinci, the Provincial, said to the many people present, 'We can read the life of Fr Joseph as the story of God in man, a story worked out by God, and lived with full human co-operation.' And Chiara Lubich after his death wrote the following, which sums up what he meant to so many:

Thank you, Fr Savastano, for the example you have given by your life. Thank you for your example in how you passed to the other life. For us and for many, you have shown God's infinite mercy, encouraging us to hope all and to forgive all. You were God's instrument to solve many of our desperate problems, to shed light on our doubts and to soothe away anguish. You were a true priest, an authentic religious, a living image of the Good Shepherd, a witness to Mother Church. We shall never forget you. You have gone to him who repays us in the same measure that we give: you have gone, therefore, straight to the heart of God. Remember each of us and still do for everyone all you did while you were on earth.

Jonathan Cotton OSB

CONTENTS

Introduction   13

I The Founders Today: a Gift and a Challenge for our Time

The Call to live the Founders (Fr Jesus Castellano Cervera OCD)   19

II The Formation of Religious: Demands and Expectations

What Kind of Formation and for What Kind of Religious Life? (Fr Calisto Vandrame MI)   45

The Community with Christ the Teacher: the Place for Formation (Fr Marcello Zago DMI)   54

The Mystery of Vocation and Ongoing Formation (Some Reflections) (Frere Jean Bulteau FSG)   64

Experiences   67

III The Paschal Mystery in Religious Formation

'Clothe yourselves with Christ' (Fr Bonaventure Marinelli OFM Cap.)   75

The Paschal Mystery in Religious Formation (Fr Fabio Ciardi OMI)   82

Experiences   110

IV Contributions towards the Integrated Formation of the Person

Many in One Body (Fr Bonaventure Marinelli OFM Cap.)   123

Contributions towards the Integrated Formation of the Person (Fr Amadeo Ferrari OFM Conv.)   131

Experiences   154

V The Dynamics of Growth in the Spirit

To grow to the measure of the stature of Christ (Fr Bonaventure Marinelli OFM Cap.)   168

Spiritual Growth in the Formation Journey (Fr Sante Bisignano OMI)   173

VI The Spirituality of the Focolare Movement and Religious Life (Chiara Lubich)

VI The Spirituality of the Focolare Movement and Religious Life (Chiara Lubich)   202

Appendix

The Spirituality of Unity and the Renewal of Religious Life (Fr Tony Bisset)   215

Introduction

The question of formation is one of extreme importance and urgency for religious communities today. It would be a great mistake for any order simply to ask: how can we attract modern young people to our way of life, and persuade them to commit themselves permanently to it? That would be far too limited and partial a formulation of the question. The issue at stake is much wider and deeper: how can religious communities today learn to be more open and responsive to the working of the Holy Spirit, to be more true to the initial inspiration of their founders, and better able to live out that inspiration in the context of the modern world and modern Church? In short, it is a question of identity: once a community has a true and living sense of who and what it is, then the question of vocations will fall into place, and also the question of training and formation, since this is just a particular aspect of that radical renewal needing to be undergone by the community as a whole.

It should be obvious that there is no simple, ready-made answer to any of this. The answer can be found only gradually and progressively, by a process of growth and exploration. Those involved in the formation of religious are faced with questions posed by a new generation, and are involved with them in the search. On the one hand there has to be fidelity to tradition, trying to identify the permanent values, and on the other hand, openness to change and adaptation, and also to the unforseen and unexpected, which manifest the presence and activity of the Holy Spirit. Thus the search for an answer takes on the character of a quest or adventure which never reaches a definitive goal but will continue as long as the religious order or community is alive at all. The quest, the adventure, the answer progressively discovered or revealed – these will naturally differ from one order or community to another, and each has to find its own way. Nevertheless as members of the Church, all are animated by the same Spirit, and the quest, though differing in detail in each individual case, will nevertheless display certain common features. What this means in practice is that there is need for dialogue between various communities on the subject of renewal and formation – a sharing of views and experiences.

It was the awareness of this need that led to the planning of an International Congress for religious on the theme of formation, held in January 1988. The papers that follow were almost all given during the course of this Congress, the title of which, 'Growing Together in Christ', summed up the aspirations of all who attended.

More than six hundred religious were there, from fifty different countries, coming from seventy religious orders, a truly international gathering. The Congress's originality, however, was not just a matter of the participation of religious from such varied backgrounds and orders. It was in its style, in the atmosphere of communion of life among all who were present. Everyone felt at ease, as if in the home of Mary, mother of each one of us, and the balanced programme on each of the three days attempted to harmonize talks on abstract themes and spirituality, with meditations on the Word of Life (following the practice of the Focolare Movement of taking a phrase from scripture and trying to live it for a given period), with moments of liturgical prayer and, as the high point, the eucharistic celebration. But above all the Congress was the fruit of an experience of life shared by all who were present.

The Congress was organized by religious who are involved in the Focolare and who have found that the Movement's spirituality of unity not only fosters a deep communion among them, but also enlightens their understanding of their own founders and helps them to live their specific charisms. In particular the Congress was organized by the men's centre for religious involved with the Focolare Movement, that is, a small group of religious who have been given permission by their Superiors to work for all the religious in touch with the Focolare. Although the Congress was aimed at men religious, it was also attended by a fairly large group of sisters, a sign of the contemporary nature of the religious vocation for both men and women in the Church. Indeed the note of universality characterized the Congress. Being rooted in the

14

Gospel, the application of its ideas is relevant to everyone, and in fact they speak in many ways also to a much broader audience, to people who are not at all called to the religious life in the strict sense.

Since the original meeting, the Congress has subsequently been repeated on a smaller scale in many countries. But the universal appeal of the Congress is made accessible to a far wider audience through the publication of all the original papers, together with some additional material, in the present volume, which has the additional value of offering the fruit of an experience with a more European and international flavour than is often available in English.

It is perhaps this element of experience that above all gives particular weight to the papers in this volume. What they offer is not disembodied theorizing, but rather conclusions drawn from different ways of coming to terms with the actual problems raised by renewal and formation in a variety of religious communities. There is a whole range of fruits experienced through the life of unity among religious. Individuals often rediscover the meaning of their own personal lives; particular houses and even entire provinces that were dead are born again; new initiatives of every sort are taken in accordance with the particular charism of the founder and with the promptings of the Holy Spirit in the modern age.

It may be useful, however, before reading the papers in this book to have some idea of the life and experience of the contributors, especially as it is this that has given rise to their thoughts. A series of brief summaries follows:

Fr. Bonaventura Marinelli OFM Cap. He has a licence in Scripture studies, is the ex-Provincial of his province, and is now in charge of the Focolare's School for Religious at Loppiano, near Florence, in Italy, attended by people of all orders who want to deepen their knowledge, as religious, of the spirit and life of unity.

Fr Jesus Castellano Cervera OCD is professor of Spiritual Theology at the Teresianum, Rome. His concern is to call upon communities to return to the spirit of their founders.

Fr Marcello Zago OMI is the Superior General of the Missionary Oblates of Mary Immaculate.

15

Frère Jean Bulteau FSG at the time of the Congress was the Superior General of the Little Brothers of St Gabriel. His concern is with the spiritual dimension of formation, leading to holiness and to a positive and creative hope.

Fr Calisto Vendrame MI was the Superior General of the Ministers to the Infirm (Cammillians) at the time of the Congress. His experience in Latin America (especially Brazil, his home country) has made him aware of a formation which integrates religious fully into the life of Church and society.

Fr Fabio Ciardi OMI is Professor of Spiritual Theology at the Pontifical University of the Lateran, and is in charge of formation for the students of the Italian Oblate Province at Vermicino, near Rome. He sees life in religious communities as a participation in the Easter mystery.

Fr Amedeo Ferrari OFM Conv. is a Doctor in Psychology and is currently at the centre in Rome for religious connected with the Focolare. He sees communion and personal integration as being based on participation in the life of the Holy Trinity.

Fr Sante Bisignano OMI at the time of the Congress was Professor of Religious Pedagogy at the Pontifical Salesian University. He is now the Provincial of the Italian Province. He is concerned with growth in the Spirit with Mary as our model.

Fr Tony Bisset OMI has been involved in formation in the Anglo-Irish Province of the Missionary Oblates of Mary Immaculate. He is concerned with the renewal of religious life in Great Britain and Ireland, and the contribution that the spirit of unity can bring. His paper was first given at Dowdstown House, County Meath, Ireland on 4th June 1989. He is currently novice master at Belcamp, Dublin for the Oblates of Ireland and Great Britain.

Chiara Lubich is at the source of the charism of unity that animates the Focolare Movement, which she founded. Her message was of special interest to religious, sons and daughters of their founders, those who have been given a particular gift of the Spirit for their time, as she is herself a founder alive today. At the Congress, from the first affectionate welcome she gave to her final word, there was a profound and almost tangible silence among all who listened to her. In her talk she traced the outline of the

16

Gospel (in love of which all religious are made one) in the spirituality of the Work of Mary, or Focolare Movement. (The official title of the Focolare Movement is the *Opera di Maria*, the 'Work of Mary'). She explains that spirituality: God-love, the will of God, the new commandment, the presence of Jesus among us, Jesus forsaken on the cross, the Word of Life, the Eucharist, Mary, the presence of Jesus in the hierarchy, the Holy Spirit. Then she outlines the principal ways religious orders have been a gift for the Focolare, and how the Focolare contributes to the life of religious.

May this little volume contribute in the English speaking world to the growth and development of religious life in our time.

Finally we entrust this little book to Mary, who is the instrument for Jesus being born on earth, and among his disciples united in his name.

Cyprian Smith OSB

Jonathan Cotton OSB

I THE FOUNDERS TODAY:
A GIFT AND A CHALLENGE
FOR OUR TIME

The Call to Live the Founders

Fr Jesus Castellano Cervera OCD

Introduction

One of the clearest benefits of Vatican II for religious life, both as a gift and a challenge to renewal, has been the urgent call to rediscover, interpret and put into practice the spirit or charism of the founders.[1]

The Church has made this concrete suggestion for the renewal of religious life. No theological abstraction is put before us, but the well-known and loved person, who, we believe, has put on Christ, a person who in following Christ has been moulded into an 'image' of Christ by the Holy Spirit. Founders have their own style in a Gospel synthesis of virtue, life and activities. Each witnesses to the multiform grace of Christ and the remarkable original creativity of the Holy Spirit.

From the figures of the holy founders there emanates that grace we call the charism proper to each religious family. This is because:

> — one sees in it a *particular gift of the Spirit* who is the origin of the charisms for his Church.
> — it appears as a specific gift of Christ for the good of his Church and for its *mission in history and in society*.
> — in it is to be found *a living experience of the Gospel*. This can be shared and handed on within the dynamic life of the Church above and beyond personal or historical factors, and

so throughout history it is continually renewed and enriched by all who share in it.

We have received the invitation to rediscover the charisms of our founders, as a singular gift of the Church for our time.[2]

But along with this strong call to return to our origins, the Church reminds us that we must bring these charisms to life among the people of today. The Church is certainly not a museum where one admires the masterpieces of the Spirit; she is the communion of saints in which the founders, who are alive in heaven, wish to become present in their children. Their desire is for the Gospel to be lived at such a pitch in today's world that it will meet its challenges and needs.

If the charisms are alive it is because they possess the vitality of the Gospel and the inspiration of the Spirit. Both the Gospel and the Spirit are ever present and active, renewing the Church of the past and continually bringing the kingdom of Christ to its fullness. The Spirit is indeed at work in the Church, guiding her to the entire truth, uniting her in communion and service, providing her with different hierarchical and charismatic gifts, embellishing her with these gifts, rejuvenating her with the strength of the Gospel and leading her towards perfect union with Christ.[3]

This continuous activity of the Spirit urges us to make present today the charisms of the founders, or rather, to be ourselves the 'living founders'. This is the grace and the challenge for religious life in our time:

— a *gift* or a *grace* because we are invited to receive the charism as a personal gift which is offered to us in the Spirit by our founders to live 'today' in all its potentiality;

— a *challenge* because such a gift must be made real in the grace of the present moment of the Church. The Church has rich possibilities and urgent tasks to perform. There is a new climate of communion, a stronger awareness of mission as she faces the needs and opportunities that society today presents to the Gospel of Christ.

Particularly in tune with these needs and very welcome, is what the Church expressed a few years ago when she described the founders and their charisms as: 'an experience of the Spirit, transmitted to their disciples to be lived, safeguarded, deepened and constantly developed by them in harmony with the Body of Christ continually in the process of growth . . . '[4] This dynamism supposes that it is proper to the grace of the charism to have 'a certain element of originality and of special initiative for the spiritual life of the Church . . . (it) demands . . . a continual examination regarding fidelity to the Lord; docility to His Spirit; intelligent attention to circumstances and signs of the times; the will to be part of the Church; the awareness of subordination to the sacred hierarchy; boldness of initiatives; constancy in the giving of self. The never failing criterion in history for the discernment of a genuine charism is communion with the cross of Christ, the connection between cross and charism'.[5]

For us religious drawn to live out the spirituality of unity of the Focolare Movement, what really convinced us of its authenticity was the strong and sincere call to renew ourselves in the spirit of the Gospel; to be our founders, without distancing ourselves from our own communities, but inserting ourselves more deeply into our religious families with a new love for our founder. We feel the urgent need, though, to make them present today in the Church in a new experience of communion and unity between religious families, which could result in a realization on earth of the communion of charity our holy founders have in heaven. This would be an experience of the brotherhood of the saints lived by ourselves, with a renewed love for the Church and the kingdom.

My personal experience of participation in the Focolare Movement is rooted in these convictions which I have received as a gift and a challenge from the charism of unity:

– the call to an evangelical renewal of religious consecration in *the total choice of God*, reaching to the heart of the Gospel, which is charity.
– I am aware of being called to live within my charism *a word-synthesis of the Gospel*, an aspect of the word incarnate

in which I find the very experience of my founders.

– the urgency to achieve this in the present day Church, renewed by the spirit of Vatican II and profoundly marked by the charism of unity. This means with a great 'passion for the Church' and a great openness to the *Ut Omnes* of the prayer of Jesus to the Father ('May they all be one' John 17:21).

– finally the possibility and obligation of doing this *together* with all the others. This means in the first instance beginning in spiritual friendship, in brotherhood and communion with other religious. It means constantly searching for one's own identity and being open to communion with each other. The result is a special grace which is like 'living according to the Holy Trinity'.

To propose this then at a conference on formation seems to be more than opportune. For young religious in their initial formation, as for those now in permanent formation, the call to be the founders today is both an ideal and a challenge, a call to receive and to give. We are called to enrich the *spiritual patrimony* of our families; and if it is not to pass away, it must be a patrimony of charity and holiness. Our founders give us a model: they identified with Christ as far as they could, and they offered their hard work in service for the Church and humanity.

We will find a common ideal and a common reference point if we look at the charisms of our founders together. To do so together on behalf of all religious is like offering the Church the grace to make present in our time all those saints who, through their lives and works, are the most authentic teachers and witnesses of its history. They are the figures who still attract men and women today because they are true incarnations of the Gospel. They are the living, though different, faces of the same Christ immersed in human history.

We today must be the charismatic presence of these persons for the men and women of our time, in communion *with all the other members of the People of God*. They help and encourage us to renew ourselves; they are asking for this grace for the Church from us religious.

1. The call to live the founders

a. As living words of the one Word of God.

The grace and call to live the charism of the founders forms part of God's wonderful plan, centred on the Incarnate Word, the Gospel unfolded in time. The founder saints are like living words of the one Word, gifts of the one Spirit, given one by one to the Church in the course of her history, but called to live on in time through their children. Our starting point is the following page of contemplative theology, compelling in its truth and beauty, which brings out the charismatic nature of the religious life. The author is Chiara Lubich.

Jesus was the Incarnate Word of God. The Church appear to us as the incarnate Gospel, since she was the Bride of Christ. Down the course of the centuries very many religious orders, we saw, had come into flower. Every family, or order, could be regarded as the incarnation of an expression of Christ, of an attitude of his, of some event in his life, of some suffering, some utterance of his . . .

There were the Franciscans who continued to preach in the world, even by their mere existence: 'Blessed are the poor in spirit, for theirs is the kingdom of heaven'. There were the Dominicans who, contemplating the Logos, the Word, explained and spread the truth; the Jesuits, with their emphasis on obedience . . .

The monks combined action with contemplation. The Carmelites adored God on Tabor, ready to descend to preach, and to face suffering and death. The missionaries carried out the commandment: 'Go forth to every part of the world, and proclaim the Gospel to every creature'.

Orders, congregations and institutes of charity repeated the action of the good Samaritan.

As water crystallizes into little stars in the white snow, so love, which in Christ had taken the most excellent of all its forms, the most beautiful of all its beauties, in the Church took different forms: and they were the orders and religious families. In the splendid garden of the Church all the virtues had blossomed and were blossoming. The founders of orders appeared somewhat like that virtue in a living form; and they had gone up to heaven transfigured by great love and great suffering, each of them a 'Word of God'.

They had fulfilled God's plan for them, and of them too it could be said: 'Heaven and earth shall pass away but my words shall not pass away', because the saints had been and continued to be a 'Word of God' spoken to the world, and, because, identified with it, they would not pass away.

The Church therefore appeared like a majestic Christ unfolded over the centuries and unfolded in space, because the children of all these saints, in virtue of the Catholic blood which circulated in their veins, were spread wherever in the world the Church of God lives.[6]

This page of Chiara Lubich is in perfect accord with the later doctrine of Vatican II in *Lumen Gentium*, No 46, which speaks of the charismatic aspect of religious life. Religious life, it explains, reproduces in the course of time the features of Christ 'in contemplation on the mountain, or proclaiming the kingdom of God to the multitudes, or healing the sick and maimed and converting sinners to a good life, or blessing children and doing good to all men, always in obedience to the will of the Father who sent Him'.[7]

Here then, in broad outline, is the charism of the founder contemplated in its ultimate source, the Incarnate Word, manifesting and *expressing* itself through the saints who are 'words' of the Word, particular aspects of the totality of the Gospel. As every word of the Gospel is related to all the others, all together they give utterance to the One Word. The founder saints, words of the Gospel, are like details of the one Word, and are for this reason called to live on in time as the incarnation of their presence in heaven but in relationship each with the others and all together, with a reference to Christ, whose multiform grace is partially reflected by each.

Consequently every charism has an essential reference to Christ and to the following of him, in a radical choice which has Christ as its *motivation* and *measure*, in his total self-giving to the Father and his will.

But there is yet in every charism the originality of a new synthesis of Gospel values built around a particular aspect, animated always by that charity which is the essence of the Gospel, as well as the point of communion of all the charisms. Around this synthesis the 'spirituality' flowers, the 'aspects' of life are incarnated, and the 'works' of the apostolate are developed. Every founder is like a word which bears *love* in its utmost self, or is like a flower that blooms in the garden of the Church with charity as its roots.[8] Francis incarnates poverty, which is born of love; Dominic wisdom, which is illuminated by charity; Ignatius obedience, which through love identifies with the needs of the Church; John Bosco teaching methods, which consist wholly of love and so the young are well disposed and attracted; John of God and Camillus de Lellis, charity in their works of mercy; Eugene de Mazenod evangelization of the poor through the love of Christ; Teresa of Avila prayer, which is friendship and is translated into service of the Church, and forms saints into 'servants of love'.

In this way, through the unity and truth of the evangelical charisms of the religious life, the Church is presented in all her beauty. She is like a flower-bed blossoming with the different flowers of the charisms, and charity unites them in their very roots. Each belongs to the others, each with the others, each for the others, in a holy emulation of the greatest of the charisms which is charity (cf. 1 Cor. 12:31).[9]

b. In communion with the grace of the founder.

In the original grace of every charism there is also an important aspect: the paternity of the founder and the ability to generate children in the Church according to the Spirit, through a collective charism that unites all in a heartfelt attachment to the person and experience of the founder. In this regard Chiara Lubich has written:

> The founder is a human being who has done what God wanted, who has made the effort (with an ever more total and generous gift of self to God) to be perfect like the Father.

In reality the saint is a little father or a little mother because God is Love, and to be full of God is to become sharers in the divine fertility of Love.

A founder can be understood if one looks at what he has done.

The saint's most important work is the small or large flock that has followed him, which he has ordered in a family, through the eternal laws of the Gospel made to ring out with a new and up-to-date power by the Holy Spirit in his spirit: it represents the same thing that for a mother is represented by her child, her very own child.[10]

Yes, through the charism of the founders the new blood of the charism runs in our veins, and the authentic features of the work of God are sketched in our faces. We are animated by a family spirit that identifies us in the Church and unites us into a family. 'The rule gives witness to, explains, establishes, preserves all this, and doing so, it is the saint's masterpiece.'[11]

In the founders, finally, we discover another aspect. They no longer live for themselves; at times they seem even to be taken away from their own religious family. Being fully open to the mystery of Christ and the experience of love for, and service to, the Church make them totally 'Church', identified with her joys and sorrows. They feel the anxieties and problems of the Church in their time. They take on her missionary worries, her desire for the salvation of all. They are open to the testament of Jesus, the *ut omnes* ('May they all be one'), a word in which all of us religious often find we are sharing the apostolic maturity and the ultimate holiness of our founders. It is on this wave-length, and nothing less, that we must try and conform in holiness and apostolic service to the charism of our founders: in the Church, for the Church, and for her universal mission of salvation.

c. The Gospel unfolded in time and space.

The charisms of religious life are like a Gospel unfolded in time, a Gospel that lives on therefore, present in the life of the

26

universal Church and of the local Churches. Each religious order highlights some particular detail of it.

The charisms were born gradually in the Church with the admirable logic of God's wisdom. His universal plan of unity orders everything, also as it comes face to face with the situations and problems of the Church and the world. The history of religious life is all about this providential creativity of the Spirit, and this perennial fruitfulness of the Gospel. It is often in difficult circumstances that the Spirit is poured out upon the mystical body so that it can receive new energy. The arrival of new charisms is always 'providential'.

Authentic charisms do not become outdated in the evolving story of the Church and humanity as long as they develop, just as the Church of God must do. They have the same vitality as the Gospel; they answer pressing needs of the Church. The charisms are 'words which do not pass away'[12] because they are 'presences' of the incarnate word. They do not become useless if they are up-dated continually according to the will of God acting in history.

We can often notice that charisms which originate in a particular geographical context are truly catholic (i.e. universal), because they take root anywhere for the good of the Church. They are enriched by different cultures. Many of our religious families are spread all over the world, for they share in the universal charism of the Church. Some charisms however, seem more suited to one place, or one continent, where the need for evangelization or charity seems to find a remedy in a particular way.[13]

The Holy Spirit still continues today to sow charisms for the renewal of the whole People of God. One of these is without doubt the charism of unity which is expressed in the spirituality of the Work of Mary, the Focolare Movement.

It is through this charism, a word of God which speaks to us of the unity which Christ asked of the Father at the Last Supper, that we (i.e. religious involved with the spirit of unity) all feel summoned and urged on to a renewal of our own charisms.

In the *trinitarian unity* that Jesus requested of the Father for all, we can say that all our founders meet one another again, and all of us feel called upon to be our founders today, united in mutual charity.

d. On earth as in heaven . . .

The Church, enriched by the charismatic vision of Vatican II, feels herself today to be more united and more universal. An 'ecclesiology of communion' should be the great manifestation of the Church in our time, 'so that the world may believe' (John 17:21). In the same way religious life in the Church is called to express an intense union of charisms, almost as though we religious were the best qualified as 'experts in communion' to give an example in the Church.

Where will our inspiration come from so that we can be the founders today reunited in a spirit of communion and of unity?

First of all, it is well to remember that the history of the Church offers us marvellous examples of 'spiritual friendship' between founders, like for example Francis and Dominic. Those who are united in God feel they are strongly united to each other; the unity of brothers is the manifestation of communion in Christ and of his presence among them.[14] Thus brotherhood and friendship is born among the founders. They are the ones who are specially sensitive to the needs of the Church. They are the ones who are convinced as no others are, that it is in the witness of communion and the fruitfulness of unity that the plan of God for the men and women of our time must be achieved.

If today our founders were present on earth would they not all be united in the service of the Church? Would they not enjoy spiritual friendship and seek for harmonious collaboration in order to discern seriously, and face up to, the great spiritual and material problems of humankind today? The world is heading for the third millenium and are not the founder saints the 'interpreters and translators' of the designs of God for the whole human family? Perhaps this is *the grace of the present moment* and the challenge that comes to us today: to share in that communion which *they would have enjoyed in history*, a presence of grace for the Church and for humanity.

What is a hypothesis on the historical level is actually happening in the communion of saints. Our founders are united in heaven. Among them exists a relationship of unity which, by analogy, we can compare with the divine Persons: reciprocal contemplation of the work of God in each; love which permits each to live in the other; admiration for the splendour of the Gospel word which they have lived on earth. In them now is achieved the *claritas* that Jesus asked of the Father for his disciples: 'The glory (the *claritas*) which you have given to me I have given to them, so that they may be one, even as we are one. I in them and you in me, that they may become perfectly one ... so that the love with which you have loved me may be in them, and I in them' (John 17:22,26).

We must try to achieve on earth that unity, that *claritas* of our founders in heaven, and then, through us, sons and daughters of the founders, what is happening in heaven may well be realized and expressed on earth. We already say in the Our Father: 'on earth as it is in heaven ... '; we would like to be on earth what our founders are in heaven.

It is not utopia; it is simply an ideal, *the ideal*. That is, it is the plan of God: to live in friendship, in communion, in collaboration, in mutual love. It means being ready to give up our life for the other as Jesus taught us, one institute for another, to love another's religious family more than one's own, as our founders ardently expressed it.

If we have developed the idea of Jesus *in the midst of a community*, or in the midst of different communities of the same order, we can think of the wonder and also the logic of emphasizing the presence of Jesus in the midst of different religious of various institutes. This would establish the unity of the charisms, the identity of each one in a certain sense, and the ultimate purpose of all for the *Ut Omnes*.

The Patriarch Dimitrios I made the beauty of this presence of 'Jesus in the midst' between the Churches of East and West resound in the Vatican basilica on 6th December 1987. Should we not also think of the majestic Christ of consecrated life, with all its charisms as words of the Word, strongly present throughout the world because of a truer and more fruitful love among all the different members of the religious families?[15]

The Movement of Religious, inspired by the spirituality of unity, would like to express, animate and keep alive this *new charism*, to bring this ideal of the communion of the founder saints to life in the Church: 'on earth as in heaven'. It would also like to develop all the existing initiatives of communion and collaboration within the universal Church and in national or local Churches. This would be only on the basis of reciprocal communion, as this in our experience enables us to appreciate our charisms truly, understand each one of them in particular, see all their possibilities and limits, and rediscover the unitary plan of God which is always of harmony and unity in the variety of the gifts of the Spirit. We ought not to forget also the testimony that *unity is progressive,* there are many seeds sown by the Holy Spirit over the centuries, and all this is part of the unity of charisms. It is rather like the way the founder saints in heaven witness to the *historical holiness* of the Church during different epochs of her pilgrimage, in different places. They are a display of the Church, historically and geographically present with all the fruits of holiness in all epochs and in all places.

When the Church today calls us to live the charisms of our founders, both the grace and challenge of this call have the dimension of the unity of charisms, which expresses the communion of saints on earth among us, their sons and daughters.

As Pope John Paul II said on 30th April 1982, speaking to the International Congress of priests and religious. By means of the spirituality of unity:

> Religious, moreover, find in the practice of brotherly com-
> munion a closer relationship with their founders and the
> possibility of making the specific quality of their charisms
> shine out (cf. LG 46). In this way together they all transmit
> at least a ray of that superior and unsurpassable communion
> which links the Persons of the most blessed Trinity to one
> another in a fruitful mystery of life.[16]

This then is the gift and challenge of the founders today: to make visible their 'communion of saints', the active and recip-rocal presence of *caritas* and *claritas*; to achieve a collective sanctity, and to enjoy a more authentic and fruitful testimony to the fullness of the Gospel. Then religious will be able

30

to render present the incarnate Word whom our founders proclaim together in chorus, repeating to each other their own word of life, that Christ is saviour of all humanity in our time which is longing for a new evangelization.

2. The present day Church and World: a challenge

a. In the present day Church.

The other aspect of the grace and challenge to live our founders comes from the present day Church and world. We feel that we are inserted into a history of salvation, guided by the Spirit which carries the Church forward to the fullness of the Gospel and the coming of Christ. All charisms are calls for renewal and 'rejuvenation' by the Spirit who is active in the Church. The very difficulties that the Church experiences are a summons to remain faithful; difficulties summon us to be creative, to think of new solutions and every true charism has this ability. It should be able to produce new energy for resurrection and life where at times there appears only the difficulty of the cross. Love is creative: it renews, gives strength and will unite the charisms for a renewed service of God and humankind. We all know about the graces being given to our religious families today for a deeper and more universal vision of the Church. Then the new needs we see, the new kinds of material and spiritual poverty issue a challenge to us: for a more authentic religious life and a more dedicated mission-awareness.

The Pope himself has called us to evangelize our society anew and this cannot leave us indifferent. We are witnesses to the Gospel in a special way through and in the living words of our founders, and we should be there where secularization seems to be the most powerful.

In 1982 Chiara Lubich recalled:

This is why there is the need to present Christianity in its most genuine form; this is why there is an urgent need for men and women who respond to the demands of the Gospel in a total way, who follow Jesus and are prepared to accept his counsels . . . This will at least remind us of his commands also. We urgently need spiritual powerhouses, people who teach his doctrine and show it in every detail in their own lives, and are able to explain all his words as though with loudspeakers for others . . . [17]

The charism of unity, given in our own time and, it seems, so in tune with the needs of our world, suggest to religious three essentials for renewal in the spirit of the founders:
  – in the first place, as has already been mentioned, *the call to communion.* This will prevent the charisms becoming sterile through isolation and enrich them through reciprocal communion. It should stimulate religious to achieve the fullness of charity towards which all are aiming.
  – we are called to live fully in the present day Church; not only to be the founders, but *our founders today.* This presupposes we are not living in the past or in an imaginary future but in the present moment of history; and that we are updating and transforming out-dated practices while retaining the values of the Gospel. This renewed style of religious life presupposes also a total commitment and a fullness of charity, and it is this style that the new generations are waiting for.
  – thirdly the charism of unity encourages in every charism *a passion for the Church*, a craving for the *Ut Omnes*. This was the ultimate word of the prayer of Jesus and is at the heart of the mission of the Church. Our founders, as already mentioned, opened themselves fully and in every way to the Church, both in their prayer and in their activities. So we must do the same as the Church is asking, to contribute to her plans for mission and for dialogue with all.

b. In the multiple dialogue for unity.

So we come to the great concentric circles of the dialogue of salvation, for which the religious must work as 'founders today', bearing in their hearts the urgency of the priestly prayer of Jesus:[18]

– for unity within the Church, as evangelical life founded on incarnate charity.

– for unity between the Churches: 'we need places where all the followers of Christ can find models of a life of unity lived moment by moment, with its problems, struggles and victories'.

– for unity also with the other religions through dialogue with them. In these times we meet religions that have remained for centuries. One often finds they are based on naturally Christian principles, and those who are responsible for them conceive of religion as purification and sanctification. These religions often include renunciation, mortification and self-annihilation which are indeed necessary for a pure heart. In the growth towards unity, the Church cannot ignore us in religious life since we are continually trying to achieve perfection 'as the heavenly Father is perfect' (cf. Matt. 5:48); and this perfection is for all men and women.

– finally, for unity with all human beings, especially those who are far away from God, yet always loved by him, and created in his image and likeness. They too are redeemed by Christ; with them we belong to the same human family; we have the same origin and an identical destiny willed by God who is the inner principle and goal of every life.

The founders were 'experts in humanity' and have given the Gospel an incarnate face at a social level, with special attention to every feature of the human race. We can think of the humanism of the monasteries, the guardians of the wisdom of the ancients and pioneers of a new society; of the corporal works of mercy promoted by the founders; of the fields of evangelization and mission, science and spirituality, and the formation of youth; of the improvement of health, and care for the various kinds of poor. These are permanent monuments of charity and authentic contributions to culture left by their apostolate in living the Gospel.

c. Involved with the whole person and all peoples.

The person, the whole person, as Pope John Paul II loves to say, still faces the sons and daughters of the founders, and people cry out their need, their material and spiritual abandonment, their thirst for truth and for an authentic life.

One wonders what a John Bosco would do for young people today, a Dominic for unbelievers, an Ignatius to bring Christ everywhere, a Francis in support of all the just causes for peace and ecology, a Camillus de Lellis to make more human, health and medical services, a Don Alberione for the mass media . . . The challenge is ours, to respond as Church, in the communion of charisms. We need to support and sustain each other with our charisms, or the powerful secularized world of today will absorb us, and we will be insignificant, just a few scattered religious.

Indeed, as the Church is calling for the evangelization of the whole person and all men and women, religious are not unprepared. We are spread everywhere, and often we represent the avant-garde of the Church, in the most forward positions, exposed to risks and dangers as Pope Paul VI said in *Evangelii Nuntiandi*.[19]

This means an option for the poorest, the sharing of the conditions of the humblest, or actively taking on the culture of the most marginalized. The charisms are capable of operating in the Church today in all her universality. Charity is inventive as it leads us to become one with all kinds of people, and the face of Christ and of the Church can be presented to those far removed from contact with them.

The charism of unity, while it urges communion among charisms as well as fidelity to be the founders today, also rekindles us to be one with each person, since all are candidates for unity. We are able to do this because Christ in his abandonment on the cross made himself one with the totality of each and every person, and the Lord gave his life for everyone that they might achieve unity. We can be united with the Lord in this attitude which involves us too being ready, generously, to give our lives for each other.

We religious, faithful to our charisms, are called to reveal apostolic charity to all, especially those furthest away from the

Gospel. We must continue in dialogue without betraying the faith or Christian life, but with the courage of charity which 'believes all things, hopes all things, supports all things'.

Unity challenges the charisms once again in the Church today to have an ever greater and more active love for all those who bear the semblance of Christ, crucified and forsaken, whether in body or spirit. Today we know, there are millions and millions who are asking us to put into practice the words of Jesus: 'What you have done to the least of these you have done to me'. (Matt. 25:40.)

3. Fundamentals of formation

What we have tried to outline, guided by the light of the charism of unity and of our seminal experience as the Movement of Religious, can now be summed up in a few fundamental criteria, both for initial and permanent formation in religious life.

a. Formation to identity.

The call of God to live in the Church in a given religious family sets a seal on each one of us with a particular grace. It opens us more-or-less instinctively to communion with our founder, with his religious experiences, with the Gospel words he lived, the doctrine he proposed and the works he did. We however, fulfil our task in today's world and each person contributes with his own personal characteristics.

Identifying with our founder should not be reduced to a mere juridical formality or to some typical exterior form. It must not be an impossible undertaking, copying exterior attitudes in almost a fawning way. If the model for the founder was Jesus himself, true identification means precisely following Christ. We must identify with Christ, live the Gospel words on which our spiritual life has been formed, and choose carefully among all the words those which place us close to the experience of the founder: for example, poverty, charity, prayer or mission-awareness. In order to be a particular detail of Christ, we must gather in everything, and in that everything express a characteristic aspect. At times we fail to identify with our founder because the transforming force of Christ is lacking if we do not identify with him first in radically and concretely living the Gospel. The word of the founder cannot be lived without the other words. In the charism of unity we discover that to try to be the founder completely means to try to be *Jesus* completely, living the Gospel, putting God in first place and being rooted in charity. This is a divine mould and a religious gains the spirit of the founder from it. Or to put it another way, we understand the founder better since our renewed commitment to the Gospel began. First of all then, even before we think of our charism and our own religious family, there is the *choice of God, charity*, which is the heart of the Gospel and of every charism.

As a consequence the will of God itself spurs us on to an intense and passionate love for our own founders, to a rediscovery of their writings which we find we can now understand better in the light of the wisdom of the Gospel. With this comes the heart-felt identification with our own religious family, with its past history and present situation as a face of Jesus to be loved and embraced.

The unity we mean is born and expresses itself in this identification which is willed by God. It has its origin *in the radical vocation to live Christ* and not the founder, in the choice of *God* primarily, and not a certain religious family, in the commitment to live the whole Gospel and not just one part or aspect of it, which we might think is the only part important for us. In this hierarchy of values and choices, which anyway was that of our founders, we are their authentic sons and daughters. Then we can operate in the Church today on the wave-length of what they would have suggested should be done. Thus we can be truly what they would have wished us to be, Jesus alive today, and totally docile to the Spirit. Within this hierarchy of values we can find the strength to identify with our own religious family and truly love it, amid all the difficulties and crises which sooner or later present themselves in religious life. Without this we would be rejecting our own deepest identity which is rooted necessarily in the most profound supernatural reality.

At any rate, religious who wish to live the spirit of unity must fully identify with their own charism and religious family, with their own community and its works. Then both the members of their own community and others may truly recognize them in their style of life and love of their own founder.

b. Formation in communion.

In the spirit of trinitarian communion in the Church, the identification of the person involves opening up in relationship to others. Charisms do not exist where one lives more-or-less closed up in one-self, since they would not then proceed from the one Spirit who orders all things towards reciprocal communion, and directs all according to the unity of the plan of God. A danger in the Church today is to close relationships with outsiders, thinking in this way that our own identity will be preserved; or only to remain open to others because it may be useful, say in formation, or in certain activities. The risk is that we remain mutually shut off from each other, there is no space for charity to expand, and the healthy, ancient tradition of a 'communion of spiritual and material goods' which often was achieved between different religious families does not occur.

The charism of unity seems to meet a strongly felt need of the younger generation today. They have grown up in the 'new psychology of communion' in which the Mystical Body is living; and they need to achieve 'communion' in following Christ as well as giving each other the charisms of their own founders. Their own charisms are not flattened out into uniformity by this divine equilibrium of giving and receiving, and the benefit is they do not feel isolated from others. Often, if this is not permitted, we can suppress the energy that can surge up when meeting others.

Chiara Lubich has said:

> The charism of unity gives new zest to the children of the founder saints, and it brings them together into mutual

knowledge and unity. Since charity enlightens, each person grows more enlightened about their own heart-felt vocation, because if a particular religious is the son or daughter of a saint, they naturally have the grace of sonship within them. They have, for example, the blood of St Benedict, the blood of St Francis in their veins. Charity circulates once again and a religious becomes more a Benedictine, a Franciscan and so on. We could say that religious will come to be like each other, since before religious life there is Jesus himself, whom they have in common, and who is the basis of all Christian life. But they will also grow beautifully distinct, because the charisms which God has cast on the earth are very diverse. This is why we speak of the Church being a garden made up of many flowers because each flower is different from the next.[20]

From unity and Jesus in the midst true religious should be born, for where two or more are united, there is the same Jesus who formed each founder saint. He unites their charisms as aspects of his mystery, and so when religious are united, their own charism will be strongly present in a divine equilibrium between identity with their founder and communion with others.

To achieve this, the different religious should therefore be united with Jesus in their midst in a relationship which is similar to that of the Holy Trinity. The divine Persons forget and lose themselves in the other, and so they find themselves clearly in their different identities. Among religious who are united, the mystery of Jesus among them brings about a quite wonderful communion of charisms, and as has been stated, true sons and daughters of the founders will be born. Mutual love makes them more like Jesus, and like the founders in heaven they will reflect Jesus in their lives on earth.

The experience of the spirituality of unity that some religious have enjoyed corroborates this. In contact with the Focolare Movement, each of us feels more strongly identified with our own charism. In communion among ourselves we feel a greater love for the other's religious family.

c. Formation to mission.

Identified with our own vocation in the present day Church, urged on and supported by the communion of charisms, we are called to the same mission that our founders would carry out today. It is the Holy Spirit who makes us attentive to the needs of humanity. People need evangelizing; they need to see strong and courageous witnesses, and then the limitless charity of Christ will be appreciated.

Our mission must be a practical, evangelical and apostolic activity as it was for our founders. Formation for mission of this kind however involves some new pedagogical directives:

— *an active collaboration* among us religious. This will allow us to be one family, brothers and sisters who feel the problems and joys of the others as their own, and who learn from each other. So we can give greater power to the apostolic force of the different charisms, and the apostolic work of each will be more fruitful and up-to-date. Each charism will find it easier to open up to the immense missionary tasks of the Church today, both at a universal level and locally.

— *a greater awareness of our limitations.* This should encourage us to discover communion with each other so that the fullness of the Gospel may clearly shine out in our day. Each charism has its own 'word of life', and we can proclaim to the world the unity of the Gospel which shows how all these values relate to one another, and not as it were a fragmented Gospel of each charism alone.

— *a strong opening up to the universality of the Church.* Religious have in fact been the pioneers in this opening out to everybody. Today also, through communion with those who are in the vanguard of mission, religious institutes witness to the universality of the Church's mission. We religious who have been supported by the spirit of unity often speak of widening our hearts, our minds and our vision. We want to live on a global level, and to respond to the 'new man' being born. This will be of help to respond to the questions of the young, to converse with intellectuals and to dialogue with contemporary culture.

During both initial formation and permanent formation we ought to refer to the far horizon that Jesus himself had: 'may they all be one' (John. 17:21). The charism of unity widens our hearts and enables us to give a new thrust to religious life, hopefully to do great things for God as we try to live a radical love. Of course it may be we will simply be humbly faithful to our life as religious, with a heart that embraces the Church and all humanity through prayer and suffering.

Our young people are asking us for this perspective which comes from fidelity to the charism: *communion between the generations in religious life* – another aspect of unity – encourages us to cultivate spiritual values which have the same dimensions of apostolic anxiety as the heart of Christ.

We must try to be religious who in everything, every project, every work, are thinking of unity, and are working, praying and giving our lives for the same cause for which Jesus prayed, worked and gave his life 'so that all may be one'.

Conclusion

At the end of this paper, in which the aim was to try to open our eyes in contemplation of God's plan for our founders and for ourselves, as we strive to be the founders, living today, I would like to emphasize *three ideas*. They will, I hope, be the guarantee of our thesis concerning the charism of unity: that it is not a utopia but a plan of God, even God's explicit will for us.

1. *Jesus crucified and forsaken.*

All our founders have had the experience of the crucified one, have identified with his sorrow, and with his love for the Father and humankind. From the cry of Christ on the cross pours forth the life-giving Spirit, and it is to there that our founders have gone, because there is the source of the mystery of the Church, and of the charisms. We, in the Spirit, must work with the same passion that Jesus had for the Church. Our founders did this: they teach us to do the same. All the founders and all their sons and daughters meet at the foot of the cross. We personally, and our religious families, can truly indentify with the Forsaken One of Calvary in our many painful situations: crises; lack of vocations; the closing of communities; disappointed hopes . . . Jesus crucified – the price and the way of unity – who tells us to embrace him with love in ourselves, in others, in the Church and in humanity. To become again our founders in our own day we ought to identify with Jesus crucified and forsaken – Jesus' moment of deepest love for his Father. With that same love, he will reveal to us horizons that expand our capacity to love and to serve, as he has done already in our founders. But we must truly and radically embrace him in purity of heart, both in ourselves and in all the wounds of the Church and humanity. He opens our hearts to the *Ut Omnes*, both in our sensitivity to this great vision and in our activity for it. Love for the Forsaken One makes us participants in his paschal mystery.

2. Jesus in the midst, the Risen One.

'Where two or more are gathered in my name, there am I in their midst.' (Matt. 18:20.) Let us strive to maintain among ourselves at a collective level, of religious families and of individual relationships, love to its utmost. This means being ready to give our lives, *for each other, as Jesus taught.* Then we truly give ourselves *to each other.* Jesus in the midst reveals the identity of each with his Spirit of love among us, and he shows us the mutual complementarity of the charisms with each other. It will be the same Jesus, in the midst of our founders in heaven, who will be present on earth where two or more religious of two or more religious families are united. The Risen One will then shine in all his glorious splendour on the Church, and we can imagine his one light refracted into all the colours of the spectrum, as his charity is reflected in the different charisms; and each of these shows a unique and varied aspect of his love for the Church.

3. Mary.

The charism of unity is a grace of Mary for the Church of our time. It is appropriate therefore for us religious to discover and express the Marian aspect of our own vocation, in communion and collaboration with her. *She in us* could then continue to operate in this world to direct all towards Christ and his Gospel. She is saying today: 'Do whatever he tells you' (Jn. 2:5) which sums up one of her missions in the Church both for us and for others: for us, helping us to respond to the radical call of the Gospel to be disciples; for others, so that all of us together may be in Christ the Saviour. Mary, the mother, is already present in all the religious families. Of course she would desire to make her motherly mission more explicit, *uniting us all in one family*, with the charism of unity making its own contribution.

This is a particular grace of Mary for the religious of our time. Speaking to religious in 1982, Chiara Lubich said:

> Mary too, through her Work [the Focolare Movement], contributes today with a spirituality of hers, so that these 'flower-beds' may always be flourishing more and more in the eyes of God and of the world.
>
> The Virgin Mary achieves this by making the radiant sun of charity, which generates life, shine on many religious. At the same time she invites them to contemplate the particular words that the Spirit has taught them to incarnate, and to contemplate them in him, in whom every virtue has reached its highest point and touched the summit: Jesus crucified and forsaken . . .
>
> It is in his light that many religious are rediscovering the charism of their own religious families at its root. When they understand more fully the gift God has given them, a new filial love for the founder is born in them, and the desire to understand from their founders the will of God

for them. Having found the Father fully again, they feel they are all brothers, they read the Rules with new eyes and deepen their unity with those in authority over them. A new unity is born, both profound and full of gratitude, with the hierarchy and with the Holy Father in particular. He, because of his Petrine charism, includes all the charisms of the Church.[21]

This then is the gift and challenge for religious life in our time:
– to be, together, our founders in the present day Church and humanity, so that the Spouse of Christ will shine more beautifully and worthily in her marvellous variety and sublime unity. Then, through her sanctity and her apostolic activity, made more effective by the unity of Christ's disciples, 'the world may believe' (John 17:21).

REFERENCES
1. *Perfectae Caritatis.* 2b. Also Paul VI's Apostolic exhortation, *Evangelica Testificatio*, 11.
2. There is a rich bibliography on the subject. We especially recommend F. Ciardi, OMI *I Fondatori, uomini dello Spirito. Per una teologia del carisma di Fondatore*, Citta Nuova, Roma 1982; M. Lemmonnier, *Riflessioni per una teologia dei carismi*, Roma 1975. A Romano, *I Fondatori avanguardie storiche dello Spirito. La figura e il carisma nella riflessione teologica contemporanea*, Teresianum, Roma 1986.
3. cf. *Lumen Gentium* 4.
4. This definition comes from *Mutuae Relationes* 11, the document of the Sacred Congregation for Bishops and of the Sacred Congregation for Religious and Secular Institutes (14 May 1978), about the directives for the relationship between bishops and religious in the Church.
5. ibid. 12.
6. *May They All be One*, Chiara Lubich, New City, London, 1977 pp. 65–67.
7. This text takes its inspiration from a passage of *Mystici Corporis* of Pius XII, quoted as a footnote by Vatican II.
8. *The Word of Life*, Chiara Lubich, New City, London, 1981 p. 45.
9. Message to the international congress of priests and religious in *Il sacerdote oggi, il religioso oggi* pub. Città Nuova, Roma 1982 p. 11.

10. *The Saints' Masterpiece*. In *Meditations*, Chiara Lubich, New City, London, 1989, p. 89.
11. ibid. p. 90.
12. cf. Mark 13:31. Chiara applies this text to the founders who are living words of the Gospel. cf. Text quoted in note 6.
13. Chiara has spoken of this to some religious. Certain charisms of religious life would have a more significant contribution in particular parts of the world.
14. cf. *Perfectae Caritatis*. 15.
15. 'We have before our eyes the inspired principal element of our good relations, that is the Lord's presence in our midst; not only as two or three gathered in his name (cf. Matt. 18:20), but as two worlds giving witness together to the principal elements of their faith, the one Lord and Redeemer Christ, invoking in a most resounding manner his permanent presence in their midst.' Words of Patriarch Dimitrios I: in *Information Service of the Secreteriat for Promoting Christian Unity* No. 66 1988 (1) pp 23–24.
16. cf. *Il sacerdote oggi. Il religioso oggi* (note 9) p. 34.
17. ibid. p. 10.
18. Ibid. pp. 9–10.
19. *Evangelli Nuntiandi* 68
20. From a talk of Chiara Lubich to some religious.
21. *Il sacerdoti oggi. Il religioso oggi* p. 11.

II THE FORMATION OF RELIGIOUS: DEMANDS AND EXPECTATIONS

What Kind of Formation and for What Kind of Religious Life?

Fr Calisto Vendrame MI
Superior General

1. I would like to outline the demands on and the expectations for religious which come from my experience in an institute (Camillians-Ministers of the sick), which after Vatican II began a new type of formation in accord with its re-found apostolic identity. We are a religious family of priests and lay-brothers. The Father has chosen and sent us to follow the footsteps of Christ most merciful, in a mission of service to sick humanity. For four centuries our Institute has had a monastic type of formation in the novitiate and a clerical one in the houses of the professed, because on the one hand formation of religious was uniform, based on monastic life, and on the other hand, our Institute, consisting of priests and brothers, began in the era of the orders of Clerks Regular, and was considered one of these, even though it is different.

I must add that my experience as a Camillian, which includes involvement in formation, and being a Superior before and after Vatican II, has been enriched by contact with other religious orders and congregations, especially in these last ten years through the Union of Superiors General. Also the contact with the cultures of various countries of the five continents in which Camillian communities exist has been very beneficial.

2. Great challenges are put before us and we often do not feel prepared to face them. The first is that of the formation of the new generations. This seems impossible

to us if we do not have good religious involved in the work of formation and good communities which help to form young men and women according to the heart of God, and the expectations of the poor. These formation personnel must be capable of understanding and loving the young of today, and starting them off in a religious life which is faithful to the founder's inspiration, and at the same time adapted and situated in the present day world. Young people must see the true image of religious shine out in modern communities, dedicated totally to the service of the kingdom, in profound communion with God and in joyful unity with each other. This is what the Lord wants and what our founders dreamt about.

In fact the crucial questions are: what sort of formation and for what sort of religious life? Formation does depend on the concept we hold of religious life and how we live it, in the image we form and project of a religious, which must correspond to the plan of God.

The plan of God in outline is put before us by the second Vatican Council. Here we are offered a new vision of the Church which results in important changes in religious life. It has also indicated the way for renewal and up-dating, inviting us to return to the sources of the Gospel and to the original inspiration of the founders, and at the same time to look carefully at things as they are so that our institutes may be adapted to the changing conditions of time and place.

3. We need people in formation who are aware of the world from which our young people come and to which they will be sent. We know that this world is no longer a cultural unity, but is criss-crossed by various cultures and ideologies that claim a monopoly of the truth. The result, especially in the minds of the young, is that all ideas and doctrines are relative. No longer are values accepted on the strength of authority and tradition. One only believes what seems good, just and true on the basis of personal experience, even if that has been inadequate. Thus not only are institutions and structures put in question, but the very notion of humanity, from which the diversity of

46

cultures originates, is confused and contradictory.

On the other hand today's world emphasizes some values which Vatican II has taken and developed in the light of the Word of God. These are essential for any pastoral approach towards the new generation. Among these are values linked to the dignity of the human person and the community, like freedom; the personal responsibility of every individual for what he or she does, even if under orders; the right of people to participate in decisions made about them; one's co-responsibility for the conduct of the group to which one belongs; the equality of rights and duties between the members of the same community; dialogue; justice; fraternity; love and peace.

4. Keeping all this in mind, those in formation must begin from preliminary human values, which however, cannot be taken for granted. Otherwise they would be building the house starting from the second or third floor. Naturally these values are enlightened and strengthened by the Christian vision of humanity.

Today we feel more than ever the need to have religious who, first and foremost, are free and responsible, with all those qualities of mind and heart which are required from every honest citizen who respects the rights and is attentive to the needs of others. Without this basic honesty and maturity the building collapses.

We want adult religious who are involved in the situation in which they are living, capable of taking their own lives in their hands and making it a gift for others. We want religious who accept responsibilities fully and freely, who are free even from themselves, who do not leave the serpent to decide for them as did Adam and Eve, but who know before God and with others how to discern for the good of the world; and who then persevere to the end. (cf. Luke 9:62)

5. Then, strange as this may seem, we want religious who are Christians; that is who put love of their neighbour in the first place (*ante omnia et super omnia*), even before doctrine and discipline and many other 'absolutely necessary'

virtues, but which without charity lead to nothing (cf. I Cor. 13). (Some religious are specialists in these virtues, and woe betide the member of the community who does not act according to their type of sanctity!) Vatican II has reminded us that holiness does not consist in long prayers, nor in wearing out the body, but in love. Moreover, the recent Synod of Bishops has added, in its message to the people of God: 'The Spirit is revealing to us more clearly that today holiness is not possible without commitment for justice, without solidarity with the poor and the oppressed'.

6. We come now to what is more specifically the religious life as such. I would like to bring back to mind an indication of Vatican II which opens new horizons not yet fully explored. It is that of the variety of gifts and charisms which the Holy Spirit has raised up and continues to foster in the Church. These gifts and charisms are to be respected and cannot be reduced to a single or uniform model. In *Perfectae Caritatis* no.8 the newness of many Institutes of apostolic life is brought to light. These make up so-called modern religious life, in which the apostolate is part of its actual nature. There is for them a very special way of following Christ, of living in union with God and of practising the spiritual life. Their identity comes from being chosen and sent like Christ, following Christ, in the same mission as Christ, exactly like the Apostles: 'as the Father has sent me, even so I send you' (John 20:21). Referring to the first call of the Apostles, Mark says that Jesus called them to be his companions and to be sent out (cf. Mark 3:13–14).

Failure to understand this newness has lead many religious for a long time to feel divided between prayer and apostolic work, between action and contemplation. They have wanted to put together the new apostolic commitments which flowed from mission and traditional contemplation (*contemplata aliis tradere*). This produced an unhealthy dichotomy which took away interior peace and which could not be healed simply by increasing the hours dedicated to prayer in proportion to the hours dedicated to work. They felt they were monks in mission, as if the apostolate was a secondary commitment, instead of being a new generation of religious in mission, in virtue of their call and consecration itself.

If we take mission (in the theological sense as it is presented in LG nos. 3 – 4, AG nos. 2 – 5) as the fundamental element from which, around which and for which the life and activity of the religious community is organized, then the life of the consecrated person is unified, action does indeed become contemplation, without of course excluding, and even at times demanding, prolonged times of solitude with the Lord and of communitarian liturgy.

For this type of religious life above all, we need trained personnel for formation who will prepare us to live and carry out mission in permanent communion with God and with the Church, in shared action with the Father, one with Christ, guided by the Spirit, at the service of mankind. I hope they will be able to teach us to be contemplative in action, like our founder, St Camillus de Lellis, who used to go into ecstasy while serving the sick and often said to his religious: 'I do not believe in devotion which prevents practical charity'.

Another suggestion of Vatican II is to give value to the person in his or her total being, in his or her bodily existence and in his or her dignity as a child of God. It is not by becoming less human that we become more religious.

It is not at the expense of the human that the divine grows, not by cutting off the legs that wings appear. A misunderstood *kenosis* can make an empty shell of a religious. Certain concepts of humility and obedience reduce a person to eternal childhood, incapable of undertaking great things for the kingdom, nor of letting the Lord work miracles in the religious. In a similar way a certain type of education in chastity can make a religious more pitied than admired.

7. It is also urgent to form religious to serve the poor and the poorest of the poor, privileged recipients of the action of Jesus and of almost all the men and women founders of religious institutes.

Frequently our formation houses are pleasant and well equipped for a good academic formation, and human intelligence is appreciated more than anything else. But the qualities of the heart are forgotten sometimes. So we run the risk of forming people incapable of seeing the needs and sufferings of the poor and oppressed. Yet we also learn the theory, that Jesus loves little ones and the poor, the sick and the outcast, and we may even make prayers for the liturgy asking that Jesus never close himself off from the needy and the suffering. So there are good, devout, virtuous and satisfied religious who live as if the poor do not exist. These religious might be brilliant managers of the activities of their own institute; they might organize programmes and offer services which are magnificent and costly, without first of all 'hearing' the problem. So the poor, and the so called 'new poor' for whom God raised up our charisms, and above all the millions of poor who are suffering from hunger, the poor we have always with us, who are on the increase in the world and constitute an immense mass whose cry so tormented Pope Paul VI, are not the first to be served.

We are in urgent need of religious who are present, with creative love, amongst the poorest and wherever human beings suffer. There they will be witnesses and prophets of the love of God, capable of discerning and proclaiming the Word of God, the Word which comes to us in the heart of events. There they will be able to denounce all that is opposed to his plan by exposing the roots of evil. These religious will be bearers of hope and will be able to say like Jesus, with all their heart and through observable facts: 'The Spirit of the Lord is upon me. He has anointed me to preach good news to the poor' (Luke 4:18; 7:22).

We need religious who are open to working together with all the living forces of the Church and of society guided by the logic of love, transcending the logic of parochialism. In this way our service will reach its recipients more effectively. Such men and women will be immersed in the local Church and among the people, especially the poor. They will have nothing to lose because they will be free of encumbrances, as Paul VI wanted them, the front line of the Church, and as John Paul II describes them, the 'pioneers for the ways of mission in the path of the Spirit'. They will walk in communion with the Church and be united with the poor without wishing to change places with them, for the poor are always those responsible for their own development and liberation. Religious will witness to and be prophetic signs of true service. At the same time they will promote understanding, unity and peace both outside and inside the Church, and in religious communities. The difficulty often lies not so much in differences of mentality and opinions, but not admitting that the other understands things differently.

8. To give such a service which truly helps people and society, we must both be competent in our field and be loving. Competence without love is like hands without a heart; love without competence is like a heart without hands. Hence the need for theological and scientific preparation which, as we have said, must not be purely academic. To be pioneers in the ways of the Spirit and in the paths of the heart of man, serious, deep, and permanent study is needed. We may then avoid certain misunderstandings and difficulties inherent in the formulation of faith and in the teaching of ethics and morals. As Karl Rahner writes, Christian faith should not be made more difficult than necessary. The difficulties should be those of the faith; not problems caused by lazy and old-fashioned theologians and pastors.

It would be tragic if, through lack of vision, and vision often comes through study, we were not open-minded and flexible enough to distinguish the faith from particular 'theologies' and 'beliefs'. This is particularly important both in apostolic work and in counselling and confession. We must try not to confuse the absolute with the relative, not to mix up fidelity to tradition with attachment to disciplinary expressions of the past. For we could even run the risk of oppressing consciences by attributing to God's will certain absurdities.

I would like those in formation to strive to foster in our young religious the love, study, and research of the truth for the whole of their lives. So when initial formation is over, they will not believe themselves to be formed, but rather introduced to a process that is always open and never finished. Then they will be open to let themselves be stimulated by the challenges of history and by the cries of reality; and they will search courageously for new solutions in the light of the Word of God. It would be very sad if they were forced to stop on the journey through a lack of fuel; that is what happens in effect when we are lazy and repeat old replies to new problems. It means that they have distanced themselves increasingly from the intellectual life of the Church, and they will cause more suffering than necessary to the poor people. There are too many souls in anguish upset by simplistic confessors and counsellors, as rigid as they are ignorant (cf. Matt. 9:36).

9. Love and competence make us dynamic and creative. Some still see religious formation as preparation for a form of static sanctity, for a state in which everything is defined and fixed. According to this way of thinking, a well formed religious would be observant of the laws, good, kind, keep his mouth shut, would ask for nothing and refuse nothing, and would move only when he or she is made to by the superior in a quietness of spirit which makes one think of *nirvana*. Such a person would not function as a locomotive but as a trailer, who allows himself to be dragged over the same roads, well known and tested, but which people have abandoned some time ago.

This is not the guidance or direction which the Church gives us, above all in Vatican II. Faithfulness to our charism must 'be able to bring to today's life and mission of every institute the boldness with which the founders let themselves be conquered by the originating intentions of the Spirit' (RPU 30). As John Paul II wrote to the male and female superiors of Brazil (July 1986): 'all the people of the world are looking to you, and they are a challenge to the creativity and evangelizing ability of the Church, but particularly of men and women religious who are raised up by God to be the pioneers'.

Creativity is a question of fidelity. In a world that changes, we must change if we want to remain the same, always up to date and engaged in the mission as our founders wanted us. It would be a betrayal to insult the present by keeping our heads turned backwards, and our houses and churches would soon be changed into museums.

When the founder continues to live on in a religious, and all the charism that he or she was given, with all the initiative and commitment that the founder had, with that strong faith in God, in self and in others, and capable of overcoming all obstacles without being discouraged, then such a person can be called faithful. We need strong religious, able to remain loving when there are conflicts, who stay in communion when they are misunderstood. That is, exactly like our founders.

Therefore we need those in formation who, far from immunizing our young against a creative spirit, will take care to educate them in dynamic faithfulness; they will be able to understand the new ways of the Spirit and this will ensure they will not miss the onward train of history.

10. I want to conclude by reflecting on Mary, the perfect model of dynamic faithfulness, who was always open to the new and utterly surprising Word of God. John Paul II said to the priests and religious in Venezuela (January 1985): "in the virgin of the *Magnificat* there were two outstanding aspects of faithfulness, which belong also to your vocation: a fidelity to God and his project of merciful love, and a fidelity to his people. May you also be faithful to God and his plans and be faithful to your people'.

The Community with Christ the Teacher: The Place for Formation

Fr Marcello Zago OMI
Superior General

1. Introduction

1.1 At different times of my life I have worked and lived
in formation communities and in quite different surroundings: in the minor seminary in Laos (1961–1962) and in a
vocations centre (1971–1972), in the International Scholasticate in Rome (1966–1970) and in the Italian scholasticate
(1981–1986). A large part of my life has been spent in touch
with formation. I must acknowledge that the young people
have inspired me:

– to remain young in outlook;
– to understand the problems and demands of persons and
their emerging culture;
– to have a deeper understanding of my own identity, of the
charism I have received and lived, so as to be more authentic
both for them and for myself;
– to prioritize my values and not to make them absolute
especially when stating them.

It is thanks to these young people that I have a new understanding of community and the demands made by unity
(especially in my contacts with another house of formation,
that of Marino, the novitiative house for the Italian province).

1.2 As superior general, I give priority to formation, because of an acquired sensitivity to the problem and because of its importance at the present time. I began my visits by going to the house of formation in the province with most aspirants, Poland. In all my visits throughout the congregation I give priority to the houses of formation. I meet with the young people and their formators. The method I use to create mutual communion and unity is simple: I share their experiences, I allow myself to be challenged by their questions, I suggest some of the basic lines to be followed and the demands to be made.

1.3 From this first year of visiting throughout the world (21 countries in 4 continents), during which I have been to 45 formation houses, some constant factors emerge:

a) *the young people* are willing and open, even though their Christian and human formation is somewhat weak. They have a longing for community and a thirst for unity, even if they have some difficulty in living it;

b) *the formators* are few in number and often unprepared. Often they have difficulty in getting on the same wavelength as the young people so as to create an atmosphere of mutual trust. Their companionship with the young people, which should start from their situation and their needs and be directed towards the goal of their own charism, is often inadequate.

1.4 From my experience as the young father of a family with almost 6,000 members, of whom 800 are in first formation, I see four elements which are evident priorities in formation at the present time:

– the rediscovery of what it means to live in a religious community;
– providing travelling companions for the young people on their journey from their existing situation towards integration in the dimensions of our charism;
– the preparation of formators;
– the rediscovering of the centrality of Christ in our lives.

We are dealing here mainly with first formation. However, it is also valid for the ongoing formation of religious, which should be a means of discovering that sanctity to which all of us are called and for which we undertake to work throughout our lives and in community.

2. Discovering and living community

2.1 *The Ultimate purpose of community*

The religious community may be considered under different aspects. Of its nature, however, it is the place/atmosphere, the laboratory/workshop, in which Christians make their *commitment* together to follow Christ in a radical way and/or be involved in an aspect of his mission. The inner vocation of a community is the shared commitment to become saints, to integral growth in Christ, right to the point of attainment of full growth in him (cf. I Pet. 2:5). We have only to explore the experience of the founders to understand this aim and objective. Even when the immediate purpose of the foundation was of an apostolic nature, the community was felt to be the atmosphere and the means to become saints so as to be fitting instruments for the mission of Christ.

2.2 *Dimensions of the community*

Community may be understood in different ways, some of which are merely external forms and sometimes mere caricatures of the reality. The community may be understood as the house, that is, as the sharing of the very basic needs of shelter and food. It may also be understood as the sharing of a way of life, such as the sharing of a timetable and religious duties. Again, it may be understood as providing strategic support for some work, as in the case of a pastoral or missionary team. Better still, however, the community can

56

be understood to be an *'ensemble'* of relationships for the integral growth of the members in which the demands of faith, of the apostolate, of vision, of psychology and so on are necessarily to be shared with each other. This sharing must be made possible according to the nature of the community. The sharing of faith may, for example, find its expression in various forms of prayer and witness, some helpful, some not so helpful: in the breviary, in the Mass, by prayers of intercession, or by example, and so on. Today there is the need to give explicit witness of one's own experience of God. It is important to find suitable methods to express this, and the correct way for growth respecting the Church's hierarchy (with reference, for instance, to the Eucharist and the Word of God), the charism of the individual institute (so the breviary for the Benedictines) and the requirements of individuals according to their different stages of development. The same can be said for the apostolate, human support and intellectual needs.

2.3 *The theological foundation for community*

The religious community is not mainly concerned with group dynamics nor with psycho-social participation in a certain project. It means especially communion-unity, springing from *agape*, which is human-divine love. It is founded on Christ himself present in the midst of those who come together in his name (cf. Matt. 18:20). It is charity which unites the community and is the life-giving support of its relationships. This charity is a gift of God being received and transmitted and it finds expression by down to earth love of one's fellow, which is not the love of flesh and blood depending on personal taste or choice, but is given by the Lord and is his personal presence.

This sort of charity becomes sacramental in Christ, it makes Christ present in the midst of the community. Thus Christ becomes the centre of the community. He becomes its dynamic force and its builder. It is especially because Christ is present through mutual charity that the community becomes by its very nature formative and sanctifying.

2.4 *Shared responsibility in community*

The community is a gift, a grace, which is received and built up day by day through the contribution of each member. Each one builds the community in concrete charity towards all the members, in his or her own contribution in answer to the different needs. Each one is responsible for the life of the community and of each of its members. The community is the result of shared responsibility exercised by its members, and of what each makes it to be by his or her own activity and person. The real community, however, built in the name and in the love of Christ, is not merely a synthesis of the life and activity of the members. Because Christ is present it is much more than that and it has its own sacramentality. It is a sign perceptible from without, even by non-believers. It is an instrument of grace for its members and for the milieu in which it is situated. The community is not something static. It is renewed with each new member. Every new situation and especially every new member require a fresh balance to be found within the community. As the unity of hearts and minds grows, the presence of Christ becomes more active and evident and his mission breaks forth irresistibly from it, as is stated in the OMI Constitutions (cf. C. 37).

3. Looking after those in formation

In the present situation it seems clear to me that looking after those whom the Lord calls is of the greatest importance. Having discerned the authenticity of a vocation, the quality of care for it is essential. The positive and negative experiences of the past show that this is fundamental for the integration of the charism, for progressive growth and for perseverance. Many vocations are lost and even more never reach the maturity and the dynamism they should because of the inadequacy of those who look after the young in their formation.

The formation community operates at different levels and

has a number of operative factors. There are four that I consider to be the most important:

- the overall formation community;
- the peer group;
- the Superior and formators;
- the spiritual director.

3.1 The formation community is the primary place to look after young religious: the pre-novitiate, novitiate, scholasticate. The dynamism of the community in all its expressions, of friendship, faith, study, recreation, accompanies the aspirant in formation. The atmosphere of the community has a deep influence on him. Formation takes place, as it were, by osmosis.

Within this community the senior religious have a special influence especially by their example and their life style. Comparison with them may be unconscious and yet the aspirant models his conduct on theirs. Their everyday reactions have more effect than can be imagined. Therefore the choice of those who are to live in the house of formation is important and there can be no question of just any community becoming a house of formation. The formators also have a formal role of animation by means of meetings, liturgy, directives. Thus they promote the ideals to be inculcated, the outlook to be followed, the rhythm of life.

3.2 Members of the peer group have a spiritual role in helping each other's formation. Therefore the formation of a single candidate on their own runs the risk of being somewhat defective. Shared responsibility at this level is important and we should be aware of it. The example of a companion, and indeed the negative attitude or bad example of another, can have a profound influence.

In large communities especially, the formation of groups is to be recommended so that within the individual group the different requirements of community and vocation may be experienced. Regular consultation with the group leaders or with the groups themselves is a means of ensuring a healthy liveliness within the groups and harmony with the entire community.

3.3 The importance of the Superior's effect on the aspirant is often underestimated but it is very important in the process of full and integral growth. Without this influence the aspirant would run the risk of living the illusion that he or she is following a high ideal but which is not to be found in everyday life, or at least only in part. With the superior there needs to be a continuous evaluation that covers the different aspects of human, Christian, religious and apostolic life.

The formation team can make their contribution by looking after different aspects, such as study, the apostolate, the spiritual life of individuals or groups. It is the Superior, however, who has to oversee all these different aspects together.

It is important to have regular dialogue which results in mutual trust. Trust is the atmosphere that makes formation possible and promotes honesty in relationships and leads to people helping each other.

3.4 Spiritual direction is the best known and most traditional means of looking after another, even though the practice of it is not always what it should be. The training of spiritual directors is a special need in the Church and religious institutes at the present time. The latter have as their vocation the promotion of sanctity which is sought both individually and in community. The spiritual director should normally share and know the charism of the aspirant.

4. Formators

4.1 At the present time vocations are beginning to flourish once again in the Church, but often there is a shortage of formators with the necessary preparation and ability. I am not speaking here of teachers who also have a most important formative role because of the outlook they create and the example they give, but of formators who animate the formation community.

4.2 Specific courses are, certainly, useful for the training of formators and, thank God, such courses are plentiful in various areas: pedagogy, psychology, spirituality, theology of the religious life . . . However, I think it is important to emphasize the role of the formation team itself. The group of formators can and ought to be a school for its members. Teaching is done through reflection in community, mutual comparison, communion. The role of the formation team is not only to evaluate the progress of the candidates in formation and the means suitable for that formation, but there must also be a sharing and an evaluation of the progress of the formators themselves. Therefore the situation where there is only one formator is not ideal, just as it is not ideal to have only one candidate in formation.

4.3 Unity within the formation team is important in harmonizing and integrating the values to be learned, and also because it is the expression of charity in the community being built. Unity, of course, does not mean a levelling of differences, but the raising of those differences to a higher plane.

4.4 Formation is a complex process that includes all aspects of the personality of the candidate and the charism to be assumed. It is not merely a human project, however. If it were it would be manipulation. We are not trying to mould personalities according to our own model, but to allow God to operate his plan in each person. If every missionary activity is co-operation with the action of God in persons, in society and in the historical context to be evangelized, this is eminently true of the formation process. It is a mission *par excellence*!

4.5 In this work of formation the principal actor in the working together with God is the candidate in formation. However, we all need others, not only to avoid pitfalls but even more so that we may enter into God's plan which goes before us and which unites us so that we too become the family of saints.

5. Christ the formator and teacher

5.1 The community, those who look after the candidates, the formation team, are the principal requirements for formation. At the very foundation of all this, however, is the relationship with Christ. He calls the person and forms them through his Spirit. He is Master and Lord.

5.2 It is necessary therefore to be constantly in touch with him and to measure up to him. It is he who gives light to see what progress has been made and what still remains to be done and he gives the strength for the journey. Each one of us must acquire the habit of seeing ourselves in Christ and, more importantly, of seeing everybody and everything in him.

5.3 We must, above all, allow him to work in our lives so that gradually 'it is not I who live but Christ who lives in me' (Gal. 2:20) until we become totally identified with him.

5.4 But how are we to encounter Christ? Where do we encounter him? The experience of the Church points out various means and forms which may be used; all are different but, I would also say, complementary and suited in greater or lesser degree to the individuals and their spirituality. In the section concerning novices, the Oblate Constitutions list about ten of them: personal prayer, liturgy, Sacred Scripture, the Eucharist, persons and events, the life and mission of the founder, the history and traditions of the congregation, apostolic work (Cf. *OMI Constitutions*, 56). Emphasis is also placed on the presence of Christ in the community (Cf. CC. 1, 3, 37 . . .). What is important is to recognize his presence, to speak to him by name, to make ourselves available, to allow him to work in us, because he is our teacher, friend and Lord.

5.5 Jesus was acknowledged and accepted in a perfect way by Mary. She allowed herself to be formed throughout all her life by Christ, thus becoming the model of faith and progress for the Church and for every Christian. Mary always witnesses to Christ's presence, she leads us to him, she makes us available to him, she makes us grow in him through the different stages of Christ's own life. She has gone before us and with her we are pilgrims in faith, in charity and in hope.

The Mystery of Vocation and Ongoing Formation (Some Reflections)

Brother Jean Bulteau FSG.

Superior General

1. God calls each Christian to live their baptismal life in a particular way. God leaves no stone unturned to achieve his 'marvellous design' of love for each person, and through each one, his wonderful redeeming plan of love on the whole of mankind.

The 'life-purpose' of a religious is to implement this design of God for them, to discover and welcome through the whole of their life, and within the Church, this plan which always has a twofold dimension: personal and community.

2. In the present world where human beings are inclined to do without God, it is fitting to insist on God's initiative, the author of life and growth. Human greatness lies in human freedom. In essence freedom is to co-operate with God's action. St Louis Marie de Montfort wrote: 'If man has a hand in it, he will spoil everything'. We need to learn how to receive everything from God; to receive oneself even from God.

3. It is God who calls, leads and sends, speaking to the heart through various mediators: persons, events, the environment and so on. A person accepts, adheres, commits self, while sustained by the witness and enlightened by the advice of guides, or those in formation.

4. Of course some members of our institutes are in charge of initial formation, but all of us are involved in it. We all play a role in the formation and growth of our brothers

and sisters, especially in our own community: as confrères or as superiors. We are all witnesses, instruments, bearers of a message.

5. Being formators in the Church, the body of Christ, is to be at the service of God who calls, and at the service of the person called who seeks to answer. Therefore the primary attitude should be:

– to contemplate with respect, God acting in a person, so that they may attune their human activity with God's, without interfering, anticipating or substituting.
– to raise up and sustain, in a discreet and active way, the free and personal response of another to allow them to respond to God's plan.

6. When a religious applies for an indult to leave their institute, he or she has lost, in most cases, the clear vision of their vocation as a loving plan of God. They find the burden of vows or community life too heavy to bear, and they hope to find an easier life (elsewhere!). They often forget that the aim of any Christian life is to become a saint by carrying the cross in the footsteps of Christ, doing the will of the Father with love, expecting everything from him ('without me you can do nothing').

7. Ongoing formation is essential to the continual growth in spiritual life (filial and fraternal). Otherwise we will witness either the fast wearing out of the effects of initial formation, or apathy, or settling down to a comfortable existence, or even a lack of interest.

8. Some present difficulties: (that I find in my institute)

– how to help the brothers to keep the taste for the things of God and a living relationship with Jesus Christ in a fascinating and yet troubled world (to waste time in stillness with God, the danger of activism).
– how to help the brothers live their professional activity (as teachers) as a sharing in the evangelizing mission of the

Church, a carrying forward the mission of Christ (*awareness of being sent: union with the one who sends, i.e. Jesus, in order to speak and act in his name*).

– how to ensure that the community is the first and permanent place for ongoing formation (quality of relationships, the life of faith, sacramental life, leisure and so on).

– how to help the brothers through the stages of spiritual growth and especially in times of crisis, which are normal in any life (prayer, role of confrères, role of Superiors).

– when to offer the brothers some prolonged periods of rest and spiritual renewal for their ongoing formation, for their continual conversion to Jesus Christ?

EXPERIENCES

FR Jan van Burgsteden SSS Holland

What would my founder have done in my circumstances? A Dutch religious answers this question as he tries to follow in the footsteps of his founder, St Peter Julian Eymard, and sees a desert coming to flower in his own community.

I am a Dutch Blessed Sacrament Father, my name is Jan van Burgsteden. I got to know the Focolare Movement in a rather difficult moment of my life; it was while I was a student of philosophy. I discovered that everything that had happened and was happening to me was God's love. From that moment it seemed to me as if a thread linked every event in my life and great peace came to me although difficulties have always been with me ever since.

In contact with the life of 'unity' my baptism became something real and I saw Christianity totally centred on love. I realized that for me also, a man in religious life, love is the meaning of life. A love that must achieve the attitude of giving one's life for one's neighbour and so the idea that I had of the Church changed. I felt her to be my family where everyone loves each other. Unity had enlarged my heart, it extended now to every person whoever they might be.

In this context, the Eucharist, which is the specific charism of our congregation also took on new meaning. It became for me a sacrament that is a visible expression of unity achieved in Jesus among two or more people. Increasingly I felt the desire to become food, 'Eucharist' for the others and first of all for my own brothers in religious life. As a result I was ready to go to any situation in our religious houses, even where difficulties were the greatest.

I was given the job of looking after a few remaining theology students after the crisis which had occurred with the Vatican Council. A little later the Provincial asked me to be in charge of another house where only a few old

67

priests and brothers were living. I felt I had to say 'yes' immediately, even if in that house there was a very difficult situation and many other members of the order who had been asked to go there had refused to take the job. Before going to my new destination, the Superior told me that really it was a question of seeing how to shut down that community in the best way possible, given the notable problems, which were not only financial. I did not dare to speak with anybody about this suggestion and I left, realizing though that I was able to speak of it with God, who is a father.

I found some very good people there, but they were each living their own individual lives. I spent my time straightaway trying to know and deepen my relationship with these brothers. I was younger than them and I was able to help them in little things they asked me, and they were very grateful. I realized that they had love and respect for the Superior and they always gave a heartfelt welcome to any suggestions I made. Knowing of the 'sword of Damocles' that was hanging over this community, I lived there like somebody who knew he was under the death sentence. Then I asked myself 'what would my own founder have done in a situation such as this?' But he had left his intentions to us in the Rule and in his writings. Before that house closed we had to try to do what our founder wanted, taking it as the only important thing. He had specialized in love for the Eucharist, expressed under the form of adoration of the Blessed Sacrament. I began alone, then others followed me. When I suggested that we should all take up again this hour of unity with Jesus, it was as if a bomb had exploded. All at once it seemed to me as if they had gone back to the springtime of their youth when they had given themselves to God. One priest who for 13 years had ceased this practice of adoration took it up again.

It was as though the heart of that community began to beat again. They had found the central axis of their life even in their last few years, and this axis was Jesus in the Eucharist. It seemed to me that they all began to feel again a family atmosphere which for years had been lacking; and I no longer felt myself an exile, but fully in my vocation.

Providence began to come to us; the fathers started again to offer their services in the parishes and our own church began to work better. Life took on a new meaning around this old house which had had great significance during the first period of our congregation.

After 3 years there was the Provincial Chapter and it was decided to revoke that decision to close the house, and, in fact, the community was quoted as being one of the living cells of our Province. Not much time passed when a young man asked to make his noviciate in that very community. He was the first novice after many years of desert in the Province; it seemed to me that it had been Jesus present amongst us who had attracted him. Later others followed him and so this community that had been given the death sentence has become the first formation house of the Province since the post conciliar crisis. The old plant has begun to flower again.

The witness of a young man: Peter Klos

When one feels the presence of Jesus in the midst of religious the young choose Christ, and become enthusiastic for the life and the charism of their founder. This is the experience of a young Dutch religious.

My name is Peter Klos and I was born in Amsterdam. I have had various experiences, some negative, and after a time I discovered the person of Jesus, but I did not see my way to follow him. Ten years ago I was invited to a day meeting for young people organized by the Gen, the young people of the Focolare Movement. The experience of that day was very decisive; what struck me was the spirit of community that I had always wanted. I had to change a lot because the communion of life that I was seeing was totally different from the individualistic way that I had lived my life

69

up to then. In the depth of my heart, though, I found out how beautiful that life was, so I continued to take part in these meetings, going also to international ones. Gradually the reality of Jesus present amongst those who are united in his name became my home; this was my real family, here, my place.

But I was always searching for what God wanted of me. One day in the September of 1982 I went to visit a community of the Blessed Sacrament Fathers. Fr Jan van Burgsteden was living there, with whom I had some contact. Visiting the community and seeing how the brothers, despite their limitations, loved each other, I understood that the best way I could serve the Church and humanity was to give my life to Jesus who lives in the midst of two or more who love each other. I discovered Jesus was calling me to make my contribution so that he could live also among other religious. I have now been in this congregation for four years and I have taken my simple vows. Four other men entered after me so now there are six of us who try to live with Jesus present among us. I think it's beautiful that God chose precisely the Blessed Sacrament Fathers to bring us together. The Eucharist is the sacrament of unity in love. He has helped us to discover that adoring Jesus in the Eucharist and receiving him in Communion makes sense, only, if we meet him and love him also in our brothers.

This life of unity led me also to discover Mary in a new way. She is our mother, all of us are born from her. In her all the charisms of the Church come together. Our religious institute venerates her as Queen. For Fr Eymard our founder, Mary and the Eucharist are inseparable and it is impossible to love the Eucharist without loving Our Lady. For him, the contemplation of Mary was fulfilled in his life with Jesus, in seeing with his eyes, in trusting him completely. For us adoring Jesus in the Eucharist is contemplation but contemplation that becomes life only in the proportion that we contemplate him present also in the brother. Living with him among us is a gift that comes to us from Mary. Only when we are trying to be like her can we hope to achieve unity.

The Josephite Community of Padua, Italy.

The witness of charity of their founders encourages new and up-to-date forms for religious faced by new kinds of poverty in today's world. When love is shared there are many new ideas; Jesus is very inventive when there is communion.

I am Fr Mauro and I speak in the name of my community which is made up of two brothers and two priests of the Josephites of Murialdo, a very small congregation founded in the last century by St Leonard Murialdo for the Christian education of young people, especially the poor and abandoned.

The activities of our community began in the second half of the seventies during the period of trial which comes before the noviciate, the pre-noviciate. One of us, Valeriano Maragno, took part in a meeting which strongly encouraged him to consecrate himself to God above everything else, seeing Jesus in people who suffer. During his noviciate he wanted very much to get to know his founder, because he felt a growing respect for him. He looked through his writings and came to the conclusion that to be a Josephite he had to have the very same kind of love towards the young that St Leonard had.

When the noviciate was over, he was sent to an orphanage. There he was struck by the great need of affection felt by these poor boys without any family. Not long afterwards he was to be the bursar in a University hall. From an environment of young boys deprived of affection, he went to one where the young people were rich in culture, friendship and in other interests, and who were often wealthy. He didn't feel comfortable there, but he knew he had chosen God and his will, and not poor children.

One year later, a young boy was expelled from the orphanage and not knowing where to go, he came to Valeriano for help. He and his Superior decided to take the boy in, giving him a bed and some work in the hall. Quite soon others joined them who were in similar abandoned situations, and so the

71

first group of young unwanted boys that lived and worked in the University hall were entrusted to the religious of the community.

The Superiors realized very soon that what was happening was like the family homes the founder had built to welcome forsaken boys. In the past these had been transformed into huge and well organized colleges, but often they became institutional and somewhat inhuman. They encouraged them to continue this small experiment.

The team of doctors and psychologists from the local council who looked after these boys were amazed at the progress they made and they wanted to know the teaching method used. Valeriano in fact was no expert in looking after children and simply tried to share his life with the young people in the light of the Gospel, and to act with them as any good father of a family would have done.

There were an increasing number of requests for help and he did not know what to do, because bringing other boys into the hall meant setting up once again the old structure of an orphanage. But we found different people and some families ready to welcome the boys into their homes – or they agreed to go and live with them. So different groups for abandoned children were formed, spread over various parts of the town and living in various dwelling places, which we called family homes after the founder's name for them. These helpers had now become about a hundred people and they were set up into an association called the Murialdo Association because all of them were inspired by his example and teaching.

The Superiors, right from the very beginning, had seen in this activity a rediscovery of the more genuine apostolic and teaching tradition of the congregation. Finally, they decided to open our existing community so that it could be a stable point of reference and support for lay helpers and young men who were sharing their lives with boys who were in the greatest difficulty.

We remained in tune with the founder's ideas, and we have rediscovered the value of the family on which also modern psychological science and the teaching profession puts great weight. That is, we understood that it is not enough to love the young people but it is necessary also to let them feel lovable;

72

to link ourselves with them as in a family so that they can find in us that sure and stable reference which has always been lacking for them because they have been abandoned and neglected from infancy. So it has been important that we share our lives with them, eating at the same table, sharing in their worries and their joys, being with them when they are tired and when they are having their rest and when they are relaxing and having a joyful time. That is being family with them – being their family!

Of course this is the ideal, and for that we don't take into account our mistakes. We have to make again the permanent and loving choice for Jesus crucified who helps us to recognize his face in every situation of hardship, difficulty, failure, misunderstanding, uncertainty or absurdity. And this means welcoming these situations in ourselves and in those who God puts next to us, recognizing here is one of his presences, which becomes for us a moment of clear certainty, because this accepting or loving the other is to love Jesus crucified and often forsaken. When, in the evening, we sometimes seem to have gone round in empty circles, to have sown wind and to have harvested only sentimental feelings, rubbish or impossible situations, we remember that God who goes far beyond all our limitations has never ceased to love us and to love the helpers and the young people with the same love with which he loves every person.

A precious support for the permanent formation of our own community has been the participation, actively, in Provincial and inter-Provincial initiatives of the congregation. The strong points of every person and of all the communities can be valued and the different communities have become involved a little bit in our experience. So there has been a widespread flowering of activities supporting poor and forsaken boys in various communities of the institute.

This has been our community life. It is similar to that of every other religious community, even if we share this with young people who are often very troublesome. We try always to put God at the first place in every moment because it is to him that we are consecrated as religious. We do all the normal religious devotions of any religious community, making an effort, above all, always to live in the presence

73

of God with him among us. For us community life is the commitment to a total sharing of external, interior and spiritual experiences with each other. We try to fulfil every provision and programme that we set up in that atmosphere of a well united family that our founder wanted. All this is possible in the common commitment of living the Gospel, and it has been wonderful to rediscover that by living the Gospel we are in perfect concord with the psychological laws, and the teaching practices and methods, which assist the development of the young boys. Often our behaviour encourages them to ask us questions and then we can speak to them of God, of the Gospel, of respect and love for our neighbour.

The constant reference to the spiritual and apostolic charism of our founder has been fundamental for us. One sentence from his spiritual testament has been hammered into our heads 'God loves me always, first of all and freely in every moment in an infinite tender, merciful and personal way'. We know ourselves to be rich in this love and we want to become its living expression with this special preference that God has for the most needy in the home – needy for affection or for correction. And we feel the responsibility of underlining these characteristics of love for ourselves by loving always, being the first to love in an infinite, tender, merciful and personal way. Therefore we try to welcome the young people as they are; we try not to put any conditions on our love for them in our hope for their improvement, but put before them what seems for their own good, always forgiving as a father forgives, and always expressing a renewed trust in them, being ready to begin again as if it were for the first time.

In Italy up to now, eight communities have begun to set up these family homes in different ways, as the founder intended. The style has grown away from big institutional colleges for orphans and gone on to sharing the family style of life with the co-operation and involvement of lay people who are also specialists in this field. So we have the possibility of doing something practical according to what modern science suggests for these children in need.

III THE PASCHAL MYSTERY IN RELIGIOUS FORMATION

'Clothe Yourself With Christ'

Fr Bonaventure Marinelli OFM Cap.

1. Jesus *reveals the Father* to us. He did so by teaching but more eloquent by far was his behaviour, in life and in death. Here we have 'The word of the Father' spoken to the human race in a human life and in a human nature.

What did he tell of his Father? Simple! He is 'Father'; he is 'Love'. He told us in words; remember the parables about mercy and his encouragement to trust? He explained by his life above all.

Seeing Jesus we see infinite love translated into real human life in its stark reality. Think of his relationships with the apostles, with children, with those who suffer, with sinners. Think of the total gift he made of himself: 'By this we know love, that he laid down his life for us.' (1 John 3:16).

2. Yet he did not come simply to reveal the Father's love to us. *He came to bring us that love, to share with us the very same love the Father has for him*: 'that . . . the love with which thou hast loved me may be in them'. (John 17:26) The love with which the Father loves the Son from all eternity is the Holy Spirit. Jesus has come to give us the Holy Spirit (John 20:22). He has immersed us in the Holy Spirit. John the Baptist had said: 'I baptize you with water (i.e. I immerse you) . . . but he will baptize you with the Holy Spirit (i.e. He will immerse you)'. (Matt 3:11) St Paul said: 'For by one Spirit we were all baptized (i.e. immersed) . . . and we all were made to drink on one Spirit' (i.e. we have all been saturated by . . .) (1 Cor. 12:13).

3. *God's love, the Holy Spirit, is creative.* Baptism in water and the Spirit means a new creation (2 Cor. 5, 17), a new birth, a 're-birth' which has introduced us into the kingdom of heaven, into the family of the Holy Trinity. ' . . . Unless one is born of water and the Spirit, he cannot enter the kingdom of God.' (John 3:5).

The Holy Spirit has engrafted us into Jesus as branches into the vine (John 15: 4–5). In the vine and in the branches there is the same life principle, the same sap. He has transformed us right down to the roots of our being, so that everything we have or are from that moment, we have and are in Christ Jesus: our soul with all its faculties our body with all its energy. We have become 'flesh of his flesh, bone of his bone'. (Eph. 5:30 Codex Beza). He has become our life, 'The life that enlightens every man' (John 1:9). Humanity opens itself to receive the life so people become children of God 'born not of blood nor of the will of the flesh . . . but of God' (John 1:13).

St Paul uses the image of clothing to speak of the same reality. 'All baptized in Christ, you have all clothed yourselves in Christ.' (Gal. 3:27). He does not intend simply the exterior clothing of the virtues and merits of Christ beneath which a person would remain what they were, shut in within the limitations of human nature. No! He speaks of an interior clothing, a mysterious reality which penetrates the person and which involves him or her so fully in Christ as to make them totally united with him. Therefore Paul affirms, with him we are dead, buried, risen and taken right up into heaven (Eph. 2:6), and speaking of himself he says: 'It is no longer I who live, but Christ who lives in me.' (Gal. 2:20). In each human being Christ has a re-run of his own human affairs from birth to death, passing through the daily situations in each person's life; joys, sorrows, work, rest, health, sickness, loneliness and relationships with things and people and so on.

In his passion, death and resurrection, Jesus has made it possible for his own living presence to be achieved in all those who are open enough to welcome him by faith and in the sacraments. In him, the Son of God, we too are children of God. 'See what love the Father has given us that we should be called children of God; and so we are.' (1 John 3:1), 'for the seed of God remains in us'. (1 John 3:9); 'And because you are sons, God has sent the spirit of his Son into our hearts, crying, "Abba: Father"' (Gal. 4:6. cf. Rom. 8:15). In Jesus, son of Mary, we too are truthfully sons of Mary even if only spiritually and by participation. In Jesus, King and Priest we too are 'a royal priesthood' (1 Pet. 2:9). In him, prophet and witness, we are also prophets and witnesses.

4. But all this! Isn't it a beautiful theory and not much besides? A marvellous theological construction built on biblical expressions? How can I possibly believe that we are dealing with issues affecting me personally?

Yes indeed, this is the heart of the matter! It is truly *the most difficult thing to believe.*

The doctrine of the Holy Trinity is not the most difficult truth to believe. From childhood on, we have been quite used to making the sign of the cross, 'In the name of the Father and of the Son and of the Holy Spirit'. Nor is the presence of Jesus in the Eucharist the most difficult truth to believe. We have been taught about that ever since we were small.

What we have outlined above is the most difficult truth to believe because our daily experience runs contrary to it; both our experience of the baptized people all around and above all knowledge of ourselves. Neither vantage point allow us to concur easily. If the Christians who live all around are the kinds of people they are, how can I believe in such a radical transformation of human beings in Christ because of baptism? In the ordinary circumstances of daily life with all its choices and behaviour patterns, I do not perceive a great difference between Christians, Muslims or even Atheists. Yet the greater difficulty is myself. I can appear cheerful, when in the company of others, but in the secret heart of my conscience, especially at moments of clear, lucid awareness, I feel utterly immersed in misery and falsehood. How can I possibly believe in all that St Paul, inspired by the Holy Spirit, affirms?

Yes! The miserable record of the baptized is undeniably real; it is what happens. Equally real though, is the immersion in Christ the baptized have had and so is the resurrection of Christ something that really happened. The fact is that after baptism we have become a vast battlefield in which two irreconcilable enemies are locked in deadly conflict: the old man and the new man spoken of by St Paul.

In daily life the new man is by no means always victorious. Where there are Christians without this awareness we should not be at all surprised that it is the old man in fact who plans, organizes, passes laws, sets up structures and finds expression in many aspects of private and social life. Oh yes, he can camouflage himself in certain circumstances, using structures and behaviour patterns which originally may even have been Christian in origin.

Our continuous struggle must be to overcome the old man and encourage the new man; to take off the first and put on the second, to employ the energy of the first for the greater life of the second. In other words we should make the effort not to live self, but ever more fully to live Christ, to commit ourselves to be in him and with him incarnated love in a human nature in all the expressions of daily life.

5. It is the most difficult truth to believe yet *it is one that holy scripture affirms again and again.* Jesus in his priestly prayer had said: 'that the love with which you love me may be in them' and he went on 'and I may be in them' (John 17:26).

On another occasion he said, 'He who eats my flesh and drinks my blood lives in me and I live in him' (John 6:56). He did not intend just the few minutes while the eucharistic species remain in us after holy communion, but a long lasting, indeed definitive presence which cannot be destroyed by any event or any creature. 'Neither death nor life, no angel or prince, nothing that exists, nothing still to come, not any power, or height or depth, can ever come between us and the love of God made visible in Christ Jesus our Lord.' (Rom. 8:38).

St Paul never tires of recalling this truth which is at the heart of his preaching and the basis of his encouragement and his recommendations. 'This is my gospel, the mystery hidden for long ages and through many generations but now made manifest to his saints', he says in the letter to the Colossians (Col. 1:27), 'Christ in you'.

The gospel of Paul is no different from that of John or of the other apostles: but he did have the advantage of expressing its message in only three words: 'Christ in you'. This expression, 'Christ in you' and 'you in Christ' Paul uses more than 160 times. It seems as if God wanted to hammer home this truth into our skulls: it is strange how it is forgotten and has not been and still is not at the heart of our personal and communitarian life as religious.

6. *The hand of the devil* is quite certainly present in creating this fog through which our faith tries to see. In attacking us on all fronts he desires nothing better than to dim the light of faith in our hearts so that he can cut off at the root any development of our life in Christ. I fear that his activities are not so much to tempt us through our imaginations with strange ideas, feelings and perversities, as effectively to put us to sleep, enchanting us with the spell of celebrations and ceremonies, with study, theological reflections or even excessive work as distractions from the essential: to live and grow in Jesus.

7. We are his unconscious allies in this through our innate tendency to remove and avoid anything which asks for self-sacrifice and other hard work. Yes! This truth is not the most difficult for us simply because it is contradicted by daily experience nor because it seems so impossible for God to love us to this uttermost degree. It is the most difficult (and maybe this is the main reason) also because we intuitively grasp that *it will demand our greatest continuous response*, allowing us no peace in this life, and (what God certainly does not want), no peace in the eternal life.

Trying to achieve success in living up to norms, laws and precepts is not what this is all about. Rather it is about being, on the practical level, in life, what we are in our being in the mind of God. Christian morality is no longer about juridical, moral precepts. It is a mystical and ontological morality, and that means the yardstick is not norms, precepts or models but Jesus himself. He sums up all the norms and is the model for all models. We try to share more and more fully the thoughts, feelings and behaviour of Jesus. We try to conform to Jesus because first and foremost we enter the fray to become Jesus, love in a human life and in a human nature.

8. The subject of our meeting is 'Religious Life Today', including formation, and all it entails. There is the temptation to wander off the subject, to get lost in the thousand and one sociological, psychological, cultural and other complex issues. It is necessary for us to come to some *clear and hopefully simple agreement about what a Christian religious is.*

The Christian religious is not simply a person who has left everything behind to follow God as the all and everything of his or her life, who then, under vows, is committed to live in a certain structured way according to a rule approved by religious authority.

No! A Christian religious is first and foremost 'Christian', not simply 'a human being', but 'another Christ'. He or she is a presence of Christ the prophet and Christ the witness to the Father. He or she emphasizes both personally and in community those aspects of Jesus which reveal eloquently to humanity that God is all, and only in him, and not in the goods of this earth, not in creatures of any kind, not in exercising his own autonomy can a human being achieve fullness. The Church has summarized all this in practice by the three vows. Each religious expresses them in the particular directives of his or her rules and constitutions.

The Church has renewed the outline of the figure of the religious in the documents of Vatican II and in the new code of Canon Law. The religious orders have adapted their own new legislation. There is always the danger of renewing the externals and forgetting the substance, Jesus in us.

In formation we have to bear in mind constantly that it is not about forming in ourselves and others the features and ways of Jesus 'the religious *par excellence*'. That would be to force people into a mould, however good that mould might be of Jesus.

We are about being Jesus 'the poor man', 'Jesus the chaste man', 'Jesus the obedient man', and helping others to be the same. This is the precondition for everything else to be valid and positive. Without this we will be hypocrites ourselves, we will create other hypocrites and, at the end of the day, we will be unhappy people.

9. Jesus knew that we would quickly forget God's plan for us because of our innate tendency to avoid total commitment and because of the underhand activities of the Prince of Darkness: that plan to fulfil our vocation to be his presence on earth.

He instituted a sacrament to face up to this problem and remind us of the truth: *the Eucharist.*

Since the Council of Trent we have insisted strongly on the presence of Jesus in the Eucharist, but we have lost something of the sense in which it is a sacrament. The Eucharist is Jesus truly present but also Jesus the sacrament is Jesus 'the effective sign of grace'. Jesus, through the signs of bread and wine, the basic essentials for human sustenance, gives us a sign. He tells us clearly and unambiguously (and you do not need to be a student of theology to understand it): 'I am your life; eat me'.

Our act of faith before the Eucharist is often only half of what it should be. We manage to perceive and affirm the presence of Jesus but we do not always reach a mature realization of our being in him, of our vocation to live him in the various events and activities of the day.

10. May Mary, the mother of Jesus and our mother, look after, defend and teach Jesus in us as she looked after, defended and formed the first Jesus in Nazareth. Amen.

The Paschal Mystery in Religious Formation

Fr. Fabio Ciardi OMI

The experts of the spiritual life have often observed that for most Christians, including religious, the path to holiness, and therefore to full development of the person in all its aspects, comes to a halt very quickly. The beginnings are marked by enthusiasm and a genuine desire for perfection, by real conquests in the life of the spirit. But as the years pass, enthusiasm wanes and this leads inevitably to mediocrity and stagnation. This levelling off sees the goal of perfect charity and union with God receding ever further.

The fact is that continual progress is required in the spiritual life. St Bernard expressed this principle, which is agreed by all throughout the history of spirituality: 'The one who does not want to progress, regresses'.[1] St Augustine, too, invited the Christian to a constant effort towards a fullness ever to be achieved and ever pursued: 'Be always discontented with your condition, if you wish to arrive at a more perfect state, because when you are contented with yourself, you cease to progress. If you say, "Enough, I've reached perfection", you have lost everything.'[2]

The stagnation sometimes noticed in the spiritual life of a religious is not always due to a lack of generosity. At times what is lacking is someone who will help us and show us the way. In religious life, the presentation of a spiritual way and of its effective elements is generally concluded with first formation. Frequently, one does not really know what to do after that, how to go forward. Life can look like a dense jungle into which each one must advance on his or her own, disentangling oneself from it as well as one can and overcoming the obstacles by trial and error.

Nor does permanent formation appear to be sufficiently attentive yet to the spiritual journey. Generally it has been more concerned with updating in doctrine and learning new ways and means of functioning.

The pointers offered by the Council and Paul VI for renewing religious life, which would have their power-base in the spiritual life, have often gone neglected.[3]

Hence the need to seek some elements which can help us in the process of growth so that we can progress, as the Council asks of religious, 'full of spiritual joy in the life of charity'. (LG 42).

On the basis of our experience and that of many religious, we would like to single out some principles of formation which are valid for the whole span of the life of a religious. Even if the requirements change according to the different stages of the journey, as he or she passes from the novitiate to the student house and the subsequent period, we are dealing with a single journey underpinned by common laws of the spiritual life.

I – The Paschal Mystery at the heart of formation

When we speak of 'the formation of a religious', we mean to refer, in the broad sense, to the whole complex journey of conversion, maturation and integration of the person up to the perfection of charity, so that Christ may be formed in us and reach perfect fullness. It is a journey which lasts a lifetime and reaches completion only in the final consummation.

1. The paschal event, 'locus' of the birth and development of the new man

We consider that the process of formation must find its point of reference in the paschal mystery, that it must be founded and modelled on it. We know in fact that what constitutes the core of Christianity is the event of the passion and death of Jesus, and his resurrection, ascension and the outpouring of the Spirit. Von Balthasar calls this the 'mystery of the centre' because it is around this event that the whole human-divine history finds its unity and expression. It is here that Jesus reveals the mystery of the Trinity and communicates it, here that he does away with all that is wrong in man and completes the work of salvation, here that he gives the Spirit and creates the new community, the beginning of the gathering together in God of the whole universe.[4]

The paschal event seems like the life of the Trinity breaking into the history of humankind. It is therefore the event which founds and brings about the Church to which this life is communicated. At the same time, the return of humankind to the Trinity is made possible. Heaven is open once more, and we are called to go up and sit with Christ at the right hand of the Father.

In the paschal mystery Jesus gives us birth in this new life, 'the divine ear of grain which decays and dies to give us life as a son of God'[5]. The 'old man' is crucified with him and dies with him in his death. Here, from his resurrection, the new man is born. For St Paul the new man is not only the individual made Christ; it is the entire people made Christ, the total Christ.

The result of the redemption is, in fact, the life of Christ, Christ himself, breaking into our lives. His Spirit, given to us in the paschal mystery, makes us like Christ. Grafted into Christ we are introduced into the relationship with the Father in such a way as to become sharers in the divine life, in the *koinonia* of the Trinity. It is this participation in the agape of the Trinity which opens the door to ecclesial *koinonia*. The love poured into our hearts (cf. Rom. 5:5) is made visible – as a first expression of the paschal event – in the moment when the new people is born, a people gathered into the unity of the Father, Son and

84

Holy Spirit (LG 4). This *koinonia* manifests itself immediately in Jerusalem: a people that has one heart and one soul: the Church, the Body of Christ.

2. *The new commandment, law of growth of the new man*

This new life, born with Easter, must be brought to maturity, to fulfilment. Christ in us and in his Church must reach the stature of perfection.

Is there a law that explains the transition from the 'old man' to the 'new man', a transition that deepens and lasts throughout life? Is there a law that explains how to bring about the demanding process of dying and rising, of losing and finding? Yes; it is the law, at once profound and simple, that brings together and unifies the mystery of the Trinity, the paschal event and humankind-made-Church. It is the new law, the 'new commandment' that Jesus gave to his disciples at the Last Supper: 'Love one another as I have loved you' (John 15:12).

This is the law that orders the relationships between the persons of the Trinity. The new commandment can in fact be considered as the translation into human words of the *pericoresis* and *koinonia* of the Trinity.[6]

This is the law of life of the messianic people of the Church, ikon of the Trinity (cf. LG 9).

This is the law inborn in the paschal event itself, the 'locus' where the *koinonia* of the Trinity is revealed and given to humankind so as to found the *koinonia* of the Church. In the mystery of Jesus' death the 'how' of mutual love contained in the commandment is explained. Explained in the mystery of his resurrection and the outpouring of the Spirit is the newness and the fullness of life which the commandment points out as inherent in mutual love.

If we succeed in deciphering the dynamics of the new commandment – which is precisely the dynamics of the paschal mystery – we shall therefore find the laws of growth of the individual and of the community, because we will learn to live according to its nature, to live as the 'new man'. The Council itself points out this way to us when it states that the

Word of God 'revealed to us that "God is love" (1 John 4:8). At the same time he taught us that the new command of love was the basic law of human perfection' (GS 38).

3. Outline of the theme

We will begin with the first part of the new commandment: 'Love one another'. In fact, this is the aspect that comes to light immediately when we look at the rise of the first community of believers. The presence of the Risen One and of the Spirit with his gifts *koinonia*, unanimity and harmony appear as the immediate fruit of the paschal mystery. The first Church of Jerusalem, the prototype of every religious community, reveals at once, in its birth, the characteristics of communion and unity. And it is into this community and into its unity that the new believers are inserted, in such a way that they find there their natural 'formative' environment: 'And the Lord added to their number day by day those who were being saved' (Acts 2:47).

The essential role which the community is called to assume in formation becomes clear immediately. 'It has pleased God, however, to make men holy and save them not merely as individuals without any mutual bonds, but by making them into a single people' (LG 9). Speaking of the formation of priests, the Italian bishops reach the conclusion that 'the ecclesial nature of faith demands that it be a community that educates with its living witness, in such a way that each of its members can benefit, in mutual witness, from a Christian atmosphere of life'.[7] The essential nature of the role of the community with regard to formation concerns not only first formation, where a specific community designated for this purpose is required. Rather, it appears as a universal law, valid for the whole span of the life of a religious. It is the way to holiness which by its nature has an ecclesial character. It is only as members of the entire Body of Christ that we can arrive at the stature of the fullness of Christ (cf. Eph. 4:13).

We will, therefore, find the secret of how fully to bring mutual love into effect in the second half of the single unified commandment: 'as I have loved you'. Thus we will discover the formative features that derive from the mystery of Christ's redemptive death.

II – The dimension of 'community' in formation

The new life that is born from the paschal event is thus expressed in the new commandment. And it is precisely by expressing itself in harmony with its essence that it can grow and mature.

A religious community looks like an ideal place in which the new man can find expression according to his own Christian nature. Here in fact love can be lived in its most pure theological dimension insofar as the persons do not come together driven by sentiment, by friendship, by affection, by similarity. A religious community is based on the call of Christ, and therefore it is motivated by a love that has the characteristics proper to agape: universality, something freely given, a service, sacrifice, dedication . . . Love, after all, by the nature of common life itself, is lived reciprocally. Lived in this way, love can generate unity, that unity which expresses, in the Spirit, the mystical real presence of the Risen One.[8]

The religious community, sign and expression of ecclesial *koinonia*, rediscovers by living the new commandment the original structure of every type of Christian community: that of the Twelve around the Master and that of the first Christians in Jerusalem. 'For thanks to God's love poured into hearts by the Holy Spirit, a religious community is a true family gathered together in the Lord's name and rejoicing in His presence'[9] – the words of Perfectae Caritatis, n.15.

1. Koinonia *and its consequences in the field of formation*

If Christ is actively present in a community united by mutual love, it follows that the integral growth of every member is guaranteed. This is so because it is Jesus himself who, in the

87

midst of his followers, continues to make himself Master, and he teaches, guides, consoles, illuminates, strengthens, corrects ... Therefore all the expressions of the life of the community: liturgical life, the life of love, apostolic or ministerial action ... are animated from within by Christ who is present, by Love, by the Spirit, by the Trinity.

a) Jesus Master ...

Community appears therefore as an essential factor in all formation, because it is the place where the Master is present. 'In a Christian community there is only one Master: Christ; all the rest are disciples (...) This truth and this attitude gather all into one, brother with brother, superiors with pupils'.[10] The document on the contemplative dimension of the religious life, addressing itself to all religious, recalls that 'religious community is in itself a divine reality, an object of contemplation: like "a family united in the name of the Lord" (PC 15), it is by its nature the place where the experience of God can especially be reached in its fullness and shared with others. Mutual fraternal acceptance, in charity, contributes to "create an environment suitable for the formation and progress of each one" (ET 39)'.[11]

The model of formation for the religious of today, who is called to live in the dimension of Church and the dimension of world, is no longer that of the pyramid, but that of the community. When it re-enacts the unity of the disciples with the Master among them, the community is the first subject of formation.[12]

b) ... enlightens the minds

Christ in his community operates first of all as the giver of enlightenment. Just as when he was among the two from Emmaus, Christ continues to explain the meaning of the Scriptures and to set hearts on fire when he makes himself present afresh in the heart of the community. This work of enlightenment can be perceived at different levels.

The truths of the faith and of the Christian life, when they are made the object of communion, when they are grasped in the unity of persons who love one another, and illuminated by the Spirit which the Risen One who is present shares with his followers, are understood in depth; they are grasped from within, reached with a type of knowledge that is of the order of wisdom, of experience. When Jesus presented the Scriptures to the two from Emmaus, the effect was that their hearts were on fire. It was therefore a loving penetration of the mystery. In its turn the life of reciprocal love, by making us live in God, by bestowing the life of God, allows us to discover things as God sees them and wishes them to be, as if they belonged naturally to us.

The presence of the Lord among his followers united in his name, brings with it in fact the entire presence of the Trinity, and causes them to live in the manner of the Trinity. Spiritual life, liturgical life, prayer life, the Church, in short all the most intimate and substantial elements of our life as religious, are interiorized and become living and operative realities.

This is particularly valid for knowing, rediscovering and putting into practice the specific charism of an institute. Since this is, by its nature, a grace given in common, it has to be preserved, understood and grasped more fully precisely by the community as such, and it cannot be perceived and lived in its entirety unless it is within the dynamic process of communion.

Therefore, the presence of the Risen Christ becomes the guarantee of light for that discernment in common that is urgently sought after by so many today. In face of the task which the community has of evaluating its plan of life, its pastoral choices, the decisions to be made, Christ himself with his work of enlightenment becomes the interpreter of God's plan for the whole community.

Finally, when he is present in the community, he enlightens the conscience on the personal level. The presence of the Lord, it has been said, is like a 'loudspeaker of Jesus in each soul' which 'amplifies his voice within us and makes us readier to grasp it: to grasp (and consequently to live) the "new man" in us'.[13] In unity, what God is asking of each one is seen more clearly, and we are more prepared to conform ourselves to his will. The defects to be eliminated, the steps forward to be taken, the choices to be made: all come into view more immediately.

c) . . . strengthens the will

Besides bringing enlightenment, the effect of the Master in his community is to strengthen the will, so that what is perceived is carried out. He gives courage, *parresia* (frankness), the strength to undertake the way of holiness and to face up to the difficulties which are part of spiritual growth: opposition from without, trials from within, discouragement. He gives joy, and brings peace even in the most difficult situations. In this regard, commenting on the verse of the Book of Proverbs, 'Brother helped by brother is a fortress', St John Chrysostom writes: 'Great is the strength coming from being united, because being united together, love grows; and if love grows, then the reality of God (amongst us) necessarily grows'.[14] In these words we can catch a glimpse also of the aspect of being protected from evil. The Lord, present among brothers and sisters who are united, defends them from temptation, danger, and adversity.

d) . . . brings the community alive

But these are only some ways of expressing what the Lord brings about when he is present in a community. One could talk about the life of prayer: is it not he who, among those who pray, is made into prayer to the Father? One could talk about material support: has not Jesus told us to seek first the kingdom of God, certain that by so doing all the rest will be added unto us? But 'the kingdom of God is in the midst of you' (Luke 17:21). It is he, therefore, who, made present and alive in the community, draws down the Father's providence. Moreover, is it not he who radiates light and enables that witness of life that influences those who come into contact with the community? We could go on. In short, the life of unity gives life to every member of the community and enables him to grow in every expression of life.

e) . . . opens the community to the world

Following the example of the Lord present in it, the community does not live only for itself. Christ opens it up and places it in an attitude of service, makes it an instrument of his *diakonia* and witness of life, sets it to announce and transmit the mystery of salvation. The Risen Christ living in it makes it a witness to the resurrection. As Christ sent his community out to the whole world on the day of the Ascension, and as the Spirit propelled the first Christian community out from the Cenacle on the day of Pentecost, so every religious community, having been filled with the Spirit by the power of the Risen One, is directed towards the world and is intrinsically apostolic in its nature.

As with the other aspects, this missionary aspect is above all communal: unified and transformed by the Lord who is already its point of integration, it is the community as such that serves, witnesses, announces. Even when a religious works on his or her own, they continue to be an expression of unity, of the community, working with the strength that fills it.

2. *Means of education for the life of unity*

For mutual love to remain alive, and therefore unity and the consequent presence of the Lord, experience has taught us some learning techniques, so that the community can carry out its formative function and lead its members to maturity.

a) Sharing

The communion of each one's experiences is one of these fundamental elements. This involves meeting together regularly, to entrust to each other what God is bringing about within and around each person: the steps made forward, the

91

fruits of the apostolate, as well as the doubts, the difficulties. Nothing is ours, and everything is to be communicated so that everything may go round.

Our example here is Mary. In the *Magnificat* she shares with Elizabeth what God has worked in her. Another example is St Paul who constantly opens himself up to those to whom he addressed his letters, even telling them about his deepest experiences, such as having been caught up right into the third heaven, or the anxieties that beset him when he thinks of his own people who will not accept the revelation of Christ, or even his weaknesses, his trials, the thorn in the flesh. It is precisely Paul who, with a view to mutual aid and edification, invites his faithful to do just as much: 'try to grow perfect, encourage one another, agree with one another' (cf. 2 Cor. 13:11); 'Let us consider how to stir up one another to love and good works . . . encouraging one another' (Heb. 10: 24–25).

The path to holiness is in fact a path to be travelled together, because we are called by the same Master to the same discipleship. We need the courage to say this openly to ourselves, overcoming the human respect and timidity that can often paralyse us. And thus it is that in communion each one becomes a sharer in the gifts of the other, and the path is eased. St Basil, demonstrating the superiority of life in common with respect to solitary life, wrote:

> Since no one is able to receive all the spiritual charisms, but instead the gift of the Holy Spirit comes about in the measure of the faith of each one, in common life the charism proper to each one becomes common to all who live with him. To one is given a word of wisdom; to another learning; to another faith; to another prophecy; to another the gift of healing: and each one receives this more for the others than for himself. It therefore comes about by necessity that in life in community the power of the Spirit which is in one passes to all together . . . In living together with many, each one makes use of his own gift, increases it by sharing it, and enjoys the fruit of the other's gift as if it were his own.[15]

We are therefore dealing with a real enrichment which increases the capacity of individuals to function. Among other things, this gets rid of jealousy and envy because everyone is brought to rejoice in the welfare of the other. The other person is no longer seen as a rival, because his or her gifts are shared. We are thus freed from the petty self-satisfaction each person may carry, towards a serene openness to the other right up to full interior liberty.

b) Mutual forgiveness

This brings us to another means which is indispensable in formation. The mistakes of others must be anticipated, and we must therefore be ready, according to the standard given by Jesus to his first community, to forgive seventy times seven. At the same time that we express willingness to see each other as always new, the other is not imprisoned once and for all in rigid patterns of behaviour. Love believes that the other can renew himself or herself, it hopes for his or her resurrection.

When these attitudes exist in a community, when, that is, mutual love is there, the individual members feel themselves free to express themselves naturally and spontaneously. Love does not judge. And the individual, not feeling himself to be judged, can behave freely, because he or she knows that even if they make a mistake they will not be pointed at and ostracized.

When we are not judged, but loved and understood, we acquire greater confidence in ourselves. The community rather encourages and shows appreciation, and everyone can flower fully, according to their own personality: quite the opposite to uniformity and conformity.

c) Personal encounter

This merciful attitude is not, however, to be confused with seeking peace at all costs, with being in search of a quiet life, which is the result of a tacit compromise or is grounded in a fear of provoking another's touchiness, and therefore in a fear of conflict.

Communion of experiences and mutual acceptance in forgiveness must be integrated with a third means of learning, which is an indispensable stimulus to growth: the personal or communal encounter.

The face-to-face meeting, under the form of a conversation, guidance or spiritual direction, is one component of spiritual progress. It continues to be extremely important because in it is to be found the dynamic of unity to which we have already drawn attention, with those enlightening results which are typical of the presence of Jesus in the midst of persons united in his name. Only here, in the one-to-one talk, can specific trials and particular moments of the spiritual journey be shared which could not be fittingly shared with the whole community. At this level it is easier to remove difficulties, to check interior progress, to face up to the state of one's spiritual life in a deep way.

Tradition also offers us a challenging meeting in community, in the 'chapter of faults' or similar structures. Today there is probably a need for a structure that would be fuller and better expressed. The whole community, under the well-informed guidance of the person in charge, carries out a calm, positive examination of each member to make evident the highlights and shadows. Possible negative features are brought up, but the ways of solving these are also indicated or sought. In the same way, positive features are put into relief so that they can be built upon. Does not St Paul invite us to teach and admonish each other in all wisdom? (cf. Col. 3:16) This is an authentic exercise of mutual love.

Each one wishes the other well, takes care of the other as of himself or herself, and urges him or her to tend to holiness without compromise or rest or relaxation. When mutual love reaches this concrete expression in a community, the path of formation is assured.

3. Love that is concrete

To arrive at this unity in which, to use the words of *Perfectae Caritatis*, the presence of the Lord, with its fruits, is 'enjoyed', the humble exercise of charity on the part of each member of the community is required. Building up community calls for the effort of each one.

In our experience the first words of the Gospel which we have put into practice are precisely those which lead us to love our brother: 'As you did it to one of the least of these my brethren, you did it to me' (Matt. 25:40), 'You shall love your neighbour as yourself' (Matt. 22:39), and so on.

We are dealing with words that require an immediate concrete act of giving, that propel one to go forth from oneself in service of one's neighbour, and that thus prevent withdrawal into oneself. We have noticed that all of this favours the attitude of sacrifice which is at the basis of personal development and maturation.

But how, we asked ourselves, are we to love our brother or sister and consequently liberate all our inner powers, to bring to full development the human and spiritual potential inborn in the person, how consequently to grow in the interior life and union with God? While living the Word of God, some concrete ways for giving oneself have been brought into focus. We will describe four in particular.

a) Service

To serve, before all else. Jesus, who 'came not to be served but to serve, and to give his life as a ransom for many' (Matt. 20:28), completed on the cross the extreme act of service. Only a little while before he had expressed this in gesture when he washed the feet of the disciples, inviting them to do likewise: 'You also ought to wash one another's feet' (John 13:14). To love our brother or sister is to serve him or her, and to serve is to reign since it makes us like Christ the servant, 'servant for love'. The servant, the slave, carries out his or her duty because constrained by necessity or by fate. Following Christ's example, the Christian serves, not because he or she is forced to, but solely because of being driven and motivated by love.

To say 'service' is to express something concrete, something effective, something that costs. The image that comes to mind is of the mother who does not spare herself, who gives herself from morning to night as if this were the most normal thing in the world. This attitude also seems normal both to her children and her husband, as if this were a service due to them. And this is how one loves, in community too, where each one is called to be the mother of the other in service that is constant and real, daily and practical.

b) Acceptance

Another aspect of love is that which leads to identifying oneself with the other, making one's own their anxieties, pain, joy, preoccupations, or successes. Love is forgetful of self and reaches out to the other. It is St Paul's invitation to become a Greek for the Greeks, a Jew for the Jews, weak with the weak, the invitation to become all things to all men (cf. 1 Cor. 9: 19–23) It is to rejoice with whoever rejoices, to weep with whoever weeps, and to have the same feelings for one another (cf. Rom. 12:15). Here also there is a typically paschal dimension. On the cross Jesus carried to its extremity this becoming 'all things to all men', when he shared in our every aspect: he who knew no sin was made to be sin for us (cf. 2 Cor. 5:21), he experienced our separation from the Father (cf. Mark 15:34), he became obedient to our death (cf. Phil. 2:6–8). Our sharing, too, modelled on that of Christ, is not simply 'feeling with' but really 'bearing one another's burdens' (cf. Gal. 6:2).

c) Freely given

A third attitude typical of love, and shown in the paschal mystery, is that it takes the initiative. 'God shows his love for us in that while we were yet sinners, Christ died for us . . . While we were enemies we were reconciled to God by the death of his Son' (Rom. 5:8–10). The temptation in community life is to demand to be loved, to wait for the other to sort out situations, to want the other to take the first step to rebuild relations when they have been damaged. Love, however, loves free of charge, it loves first, without making any demands. It finds in love itself the motivation for loving.

d) Universality

And finally, we can glean another dimension of love from the paschal mystery: its universality. Love loves all, without exclusion or preference. All! It is a word repeated frequently by Jesus, precisely in the context of the paschal event: 'I, when I am lifted up from the earth, will draw all men to myself' (John 12:32). 'Father . . . that they may all be one' (John 17:21).

Religious must exert themselves to serve, welcome, love freely each one of their brothers or sisters in community, setting aside the inevitable feeling of preference or antipathy. But they must also widen their souls towards the members of the other religious families, until the other Institutes are loved as their own. They must go even further looking towards ecumenism, towards the members of other religions, towards the poor, the very least, as well as towards atheists, those who are indifferent . . .

4. Love for one's neighbour the way of holiness

This simple way of love is the first dimension for the formation of every Christian. Does not Scripture teach us that the way of conversion and growth finds its principal road precisely in brotherly love? The Christian way consists in 'walking in love' (Eph. 5:2); indeed, to continue with St Paul's words, love is the 'still more excellent way' (1 Cor. 12:31). In fact, charity is the fulfilment of the law (cf. Rom. 13:10), the bond of perfection (cf. Col. 3:14). And it is precisely through brotherly love that we pass out of death into life (cf. 1 John 3:14). We are at the heart of the paschal mystery, which is the extreme act of self-giving to the Father and to the brothers and sisters in the spirit of love.

The exercise of love gives growth to the divine life in the one who loves and it brings him or her to the fullness of communion with God. In the Christian sacramental economy we cannot arrive at holiness, which is precisely full and perfect communion with God, if we do not pass through the humanity of Christ which in its turn is present in every person. Our brother or sister becomes the immediate, concrete 'way' to reach God, as well as being the means of checking spiritual progress (cf. 1 John 4: 12, 20). A brother or sister becomes for me a 'sacrament' for meeting with God, the door which leads me to God. In this context St Augustine writes: 'There is no surer step for reaching love of God than the charity of man for man.'[16]

Throughout life, even in the most advanced stages of spiritual growth, we must always return, in an ever deeper way, to the simple, daily, concrete exercise of brotherly love. In time of trial, too, a return to love of one's neighbour forms the necessary step to regaining fullness of life.

We are at the ABC of the Gospel. It is a 'little way', but it enlarges the soul progressively and gives the person the typical characteristics of charity, making him or her patient and kind. A person thus engaged in loving 'is not jealous or boastful, is not arrogant or rude, does not insist on his own way, is not irritable or resentful, does not rejoice at wrong, but rejoices in the right. Love bears all things, believes all things, hopes all things, endures all things' (1 Cor. 13: 4–7).

In St Paul's description of what charity brings about, we cannot but see a description of the man who has already arrived at maturity, at complete self-control, equilibrium, magnanimity, one who has already overcome self-centredness and has become, with Christ the perfect man, a person who gives himself or herself, who no longer lives for self but for building up the Church, one who is fully committed to the kingdom of God. A person who becomes 'charity' in such a manner will remain forever, just as charity itself remains forever (cf. 1 Cor. 13:8).

III – Demands made by the mystery of death in formation

Up to this point, we have looked at one aspect of the paschal mystery. We have seen how the risen Christ, present in his community, transforms its members and how the practice of mutual love nurtures this process of formation. But so that the risen Christ may be present in the community, so that love may be true, we must die to one another: and this is the other aspect of the paschal mystery. The resurrection and the outpouring of full life which is typical of *koinonia*, are in fact the fruit of the redemptive death of Christ. Because when he is lifted up from the earth (mystery of his cross and death), Jesus draws all men to himself (mystery of resurrection and life) giving existence to the Church-Communion (cf. John 12:32). Because he falls to earth and dies like a single grain, he gives birth to the ear of grain where life is increased and unified.

The new commandment, which gives expression to this new dynamic of the paschal mystery, accordingly implies the aspect of death. The love which typifies the new commandment is not to be found only in reciprocity, but also in its nature: it is a matter of love 'as' Christ has loved, and he has loved to the point of giving his life for his friends. 'Having loved his own . . . he loved them to the end' (John 13:1), to the extreme sign of death, death on a cross. Christ who gives his life on the cross is the model for loving our brothers and sisters. 'His death on the cross, forsaken, is the highest, divine, heroic, lesson from Jesus about what love is.'[17]

Let us now look at some of the implications of giving one's life. We will try to see its main formative features and to grasp the process which makes of death the gateway to life, to building up the new man, made fully Christ. We will begin from what most characterizes us as religious.

1. Radical discipleship

In their act of consecration, the religious commit themselves to following Jesus and are called to make their love radical, which is demanded by discipleship, their characteristic lifestyle. A full five times the Synoptics report the words of Jesus: 'If any man would come after me, let him deny himself and take up his cross and follow me' (Mark 8:34 and parallel). 'In relating to another, denial means not to acknowledge that person, not to take that person into account, to detach oneself from whatever bonds there are. That is how Peter denies Jesus (Mark 14:30, 29, 70). To deny oneself is to fail to take into account what is deepest in oneself: the desire for self-affirmation and life.'[18] This is what Jesus invites us to. When he asks us to take up our cross, he wants us to be ready to share his destiny of death. This is the origin of the commitment of the religious to complete detachment from things and creatures, from self, as well as from any spiritual consolation, in order to be able to love with the very love of Christ.

In the act of dying Jesus gives the Spirit. His death is for life. Similarly, for us, 'denial' and taking up the cross are to generate life. In dying through love of one another, we give life to one another reciprocally by giving life to the Risen Christ in our midst.

When Luke specifies that we must take up the cross 'every day' (Luke 9:23), he gives us to understand that sharing the death of Jesus comes about by daily forgetting ourselves, losing ourselves, denying ourselves . . . We are therefore in the daily, concrete process of our formation, where this dying to ourselves is put into practice as the necessary gateway to the birth of the new man, both as individual and community.

We can see the typical expressions of this daily dying in the life of the religious, which is characterized by chastity, poverty, obedience, common life, apostolate.

a) Chastity

Chastity by its nature leads to the highest expression of love. But so that the heart may be enlarged on the pattern of Christ's heart, in such a way as to love in a supernatural manner, in virginity and consecrated chastity the affections must often be purified. This is achieved by cutting away where necessary, by living prudently, by mortification, by vigilance. At times all of this can be seen as truly dying, as the gospel 'losing one's life' (Mark 8:35), 'hating his life' (John 12:25), because one's family is taken away, 'mother, wife, children, brothers, sisters' (Luke 14:26). At some stages this can become a lacerating suffering, and we can be tempted to turn back or to stoop to compromise.

Jesus on the cross did not support himself with any form of help, human, spiritual or divine. Almost all his disciples had left him. He separated his mother from himself in giving her to John. Even his Father seemed to abandon him. This is the model for anyone who must purify their heart so as to attain a love which is all-embracing.

b) Poverty

So that love may be concrete, even to the extent of sharing completely all one has and one is, there must be effective and affective detachment from everything. This is the step which every religious has taken when responding to Jesus' invitation to leave everything and follow him. With the passing of the years a desire for a certain standard of life or prestige or security can subtly re-appear. Or there may be the temptation to become attached to work, or to one's own duties, to the apostolate, to a particular location, even to certain people, because of the inborn instinct for self-realization: to be appreciated, considered, esteemed, to meet with agreement and approval . . . This is a means of seeking to 'save one's own life' with the risk of losing it instead.

On the cross Jesus teaches us the most complete detachment from everything. He strips himself of everything and gives his body, blood, soul, and divinity. He is the model of anyone who is called to give himself completely, sharing all that he has.

c) Obedience

So that unity within the community may be perfect and that the will of the Father may be fully done, we must give up our feelings, our projects, our will. Gradually, as we reach a certain stage of maturity, we become increasingly aware of our ability to think, estimate, and plan our work. The temptation to become autonomous in our decisions can arise, to begin to control others and impose our approach to goals, our personally developed strategies.

On the cross Jesus wholeheartedly accepted and fulfilled his Father's will, even when this meant turning out every light, even when it cost him his life. He is the model of all who must overcome experiencing obedience as absurdity, or the lack of rapport with their superiors.

d) Common life

When there is a shared decision to undertake the building up of community and to travel the spiritual journey in unity, there is readiness for reciprocal love which leads to unity. At a given moment brotherly relations can be in crisis; life in community in which we have believed may appear to be a utopia, an illusion. But this is a healthy crisis, without which we would risk using our brothers. If I set out to meet another in love and be the first to love, that is, without expecting anything in return, I create the condition for communion, which is to love my sister or brother because here is Christ to be served and loved for his own sake, not because of the joys or advantages that I gain.

Here, too, Jesus is the model. On the cross he was forsaken, at that moment when he surrendered himself to the Father, while feeling that he had lost his relationship with him. This is the model for all who are called to rebuild community relationships on a love motivated wholly by faith.

e) Apostolic life

Community helps to develop apostolic potential. It is not rare to see works developing around it, conversions flourishing . . . But failure, lack of success, inefficiency, discouragement, tiredness, can appear. Works which at first prospered can collapse, people who were following you can be found wanting . . .

On the cross Jesus seemed to be reduced to powerlessness. His community had been scattered. He found himself denied, betrayed, abandoned. And even there, when he was most powerless – nailed to the cross he could no longer speak, nor work miracles, nor heal the sick – he accomplishes the most fruitful work of all: the redemption of the world. He is the highest model for those who are called to undergo purification in the apostolate, because nobody can undertake on his own a work that is truly of Christ.

2. Growth in everyday conditions

These are the headlines of a discipleship which demands sharing Christ's destiny. However, they break into daily life, scattered about in thousands of occasions when the expert hand of the Father is present to prune and yield more fruit. It can be a humiliation, a reproof, a moment of discomfort, discouragement, loss of direction. Or it can be an upset, a disaster, a sickness, an absurd situation, a temptation. It can even be a simple headache, or failing to answer well, or a mishap, a delay, or a gaffe.

These last things especially, so frequent on any day, are what can vex and annoy us. We can see them as inevitable, and that therefore we must be resigned to them, if we are virtuous; or we can see them as mundane things, unworthy of our consideration, to be passed over without bothering about them.

A genuine formation should instead find in all these tiny events the opportunities to take a step forward and grow in love. We are in danger of spending our lives waiting for the great occasions to become saints, to live love in a heroic manner, but these occasions may never come our way. It is in the daily routine that interior growth can take place, and the person can mature. It is here that the authentic path to holiness is worked out.

How then are we to exploit what is negative, the pain that surrounds our daily life? How are we to make it a means to formation? I propose three steps.

a) Seeing Christ present in what is negative . . .

We must teach ourselves and others to have a vision of faith which can recognize every negative thing – whatever it may be, whatever its significance, wherever we meet it – as a sacrament that allows us to meet Christ in the mystery of his death and resurrection. If Jesus in his redemptive death has taken on himself everything that is negative, then in everything that is negative we can discover his presence. 'We feel ourselves abandoned, alone? He is there. Betrayed or humiliated? He is there. Disorientated or astray or failures? Lukewarm or sinners? He is there. He is there, always faithful. It is a fact: He is never missing'.[19] What is involved is grasping an authentic Christian vision of reality. Everything has been redeemed. Nothing is commonplace. From the most agonizing to the most ordinary pain, everything is to be grasped as deeply sacred and read with Christ's outlook; rather, it is to be lived in Christ.

b) . . . to welcome him and cling to him in love

In fact, in formation we must not only learn to recognize the face of Christ in every suffering. We must also strive to cling to him with all our being, in a positive act of choice that is a true act of love. That negative situation, that suffering, is not to be endured: it is to be seized with joy and made our own, like a 'eucharistic species' which bestows communion with Christ the redeemer. Only thus will the mystery of the cross become a 'gateway' leading to the fullness of the life of the Trinity. We enter with Christ into the mystery of his death,

104

and because we die with him who died, we discover the Risen One within ourselves. Sharing his death makes us sharers in the fruits of his spirit: 'love, joy, peace, patience, kindness, goodness, faithfulness, gentleness, self-control' (Gal. 5:22). Only on these conditions can we truly love. Only by living as the Risen Christ and sharing in the fruits of his Spirit, can conditions be such that the Risen Christ lives and works through all the members of the community.

c) . . . to seek him and prefer him

Even yet the task of formation has not been exhausted. It is not enough to recognize Christ present in suffering, nor to cling to him in love. We must press on; in fact, to seek out Christ who has taken on himself all that is negative, and to prefer him. Just as Christ came for sinners, for the sick, he came to search for the straying sheep, for what was lost; he has borne our sins and has become a curse for us; so we must seek for Christ where his presence is most in evidence: in the sufferings of those with whom we live, in the divisions or tensions or difficulties that may occur in the community, in the uncertainty caused by the shortage of vocations. But we must seek him also in the ills of society, in the coldness of a world that is individualistic and indifferent, in the divisions in the Church, in injustice, among the poor . . . We must seek him also in the sufferings involved in the virtues we are called to live with commitment: purity, patience, meekness, mercy. We choose to offer the other cheek to the one who strikes us, to go two miles with anyone who asks us to go with them for one.

3. Towards sharing fully in the mystery of Christ's death

Besides this 'daily grind' in his or her life, a religious can also be called to face situations that are particularly difficult, that can require an interior somersault, deep uprootings. If these are faced up to and resolved, they mark real moments of conversion. If they are ignored, spiritual progress is blocked or languishes, often with the danger of turning in on itself. In fact, in the spiritual life we cannot remain stationary or avoid particular choices. God awaits us at these turning-points of life; they are decisive appointments.

The pattern is very widespread in religious life. Someone is removed from office, or changed from a community. This fact can often be perceived as a punishment, a lack of confidence. Or there may be a real misunderstanding on the part of Superiors. Natural gifts or competence go unrecognized. We can feel ourselves dismissed, sidelined, rejected. A person feels mortified. His or her personality is effectively crushed. They may seem to be 'without personality', completely stripped, cut alive.

Faced with a situation of this kind, we can break with the community; we can become rigid and closed towards our Superiors. But this 'loss' of personality is the one condition for acquiring true personality, the 'personality' of Christ. 'I have been crucified with Christ; it is no longer I who live' (and who feels death, the denial of every chance of affirmation, or status, or recognition) 'but Christ who lives in me' (Gal. 2:20). On my death is his life. The 'new man' is consolidated. The maturity of Christ is reached. Even while experiencing at times his or her own poverty and nothingness, in fact the religious objectively becomes an adult in Christ: Christ reaches adult stature in the individual.

The supreme trial is reserved for whoever goes even further, with faithfulness, in the spiritual life. Throughout life a person has believed in the love of God, has concentrated their existence on this faith in his love, and then for various reasons it seems as if they are abandoned by him. 'Well then, even here, in this situation, [we] must look to Jesus Forsaken. Did not Jesus say that all would abandon him, but the Father would always remain with him? However, in abandonment the contrary occurs. The Father seems to abandon him. It is tremendous, it is tragic. And what does he do? He gives a loud cry, but then he re-abandons himself to his Father. Thus we too must act in these circumstances. They are, I think, moments that are valuable before God. With his abandonment Jesus brought redemption to fulfilment. We, with our abandonment united to his, will bring about our purification and we will help who knows how many souls'.[20]

Conclusion

And so we behold the religious who has reached full maturity, who is an adult in Christ and a true witness to God who is Love. He is capable of being a channel of the various graces of God, of understanding from within his founder, and of putting the founder's charism into practice in the Church of today. Already he or she can bear the 'burden of the day', and can stand with every person and share their joys and hopes, anguish and suffering; and he or she can give concrete, constructive answers to the needs of all they may meet.

When we have 'lost' our own personality to put on Christ's, we notice that Christ, whom one has welcomed into oneself, puts on the personality of the religious. Christ makes it his own, and expresses himself in its feelings, gifts, affections, its inner richness.

In unity with our sisters or brothers, the religious is capable of building, guiding, loving, opening his or her heart, of becoming father and mother to humanity, because it is Christ in him or her who accomplishes all this. Without any trace of a selfish possessiveness, the religious feels that all belongs to them, that all is theirs, because they are Christ and Christ is of God. They are ready for anything, not with a view to their own needs, or status, or self-realization, but in view of the Kingdom. They live totally and unconditionally for Christ; they are his instruments and live for his ideal, the *ut omnes*.

Everywhere they give expression to their own community because, having matured in relationship with the brothers or sisters God has given them, they have become people of communion. They are able to assist in overcoming division and discord, and to help to build the relationships of unity.

Christ now finds such a religious free, ready, and mature enough to be entrusted with the lot of his Church, with the interests of the Kingdom and of all humankind. Apostolic zeal has been purified; intimacy with God is deep and tending to full mystical union; communion with others simplified. Maturity, adulthood in Christ, is now expressed in fruitfulness: 'By this my Father is glorified, that you bear much fruit' (John 15:8).

REFERENCES
1. Letter 254, 4; PL 182, 461
2. Sermon 169, 15, 18; PL 38, 926.
3. A basic treatment of this may be found in my article *Note sulla dottrina dei religiosi nei documenti post-conciliari*, in Claretianum, 26 (1986) 296–301.
4. For a theological development of the theme, cf. P.Coda, *Evento Pasquale. Trinità e Storia*, Rome 1983.
5. C.Lubich, *Scritti Spirituali*, III, Rome 1975, p.55.
6. For the further development of this theme it is important to emphasize the intrinsic relationship between trinitarian love and mutual love, mediated by the Easter event. 'To love one another in Christ, in the measure of his love, is to live the love of the Trinity on earth, grafted, individually and together, into the life of Love of God himself: *mutual love is therefore the life of the pericoresis [mutual indwelling] of the Trinity shared with men* (. . . .). In Christ, the Church itself becomes in reality an ikon of the life of the Trinity: because men are enabled, in grace, to live in their mutual relationships an existence which translates into history the very life of the pericoresis of the Trinity. "On earth as it is in heaven". Man, redeemed and divinized, can already love his fellow man *as* Christ has loved him: because Christ lives in the one who loves, and in the other who is loved the same Christ lives. Their reciprocal love is divinized, it is Trinitarian. It is Christ in me who loves Christ in you – and this reciprocal love is Love of Christ, it is Holy Spirit. Between the two who love in this way, with the love of Christ, the presence of a third Person is established – analogously to what happens in the most holy Trinity, where the Father and the Son love one another in the *Holy Spirit* –, a Third Person who is the risen Christ himself, present in the power and light of his Spirit' (P. Coda, *La Chiesa, profezia dell'umanità compiuta* . . . , in AA.VV., *La Chiesa salvezza dell'uomo*, Rome 1984, pp. 93–94).
7. *La preparazione al sacerdozio ministeriale. Orientamenti e norme*, Rome, 1972, p. 109.

8. On the presence of the risen Lord in the community of disciples gathered in his name, one can read: J. M. Povilus, *'Gesú in mezzo' nel pensiero di Chiara Lubich*, Rome 1981.

9. J. M. R. Tillard, who considers PC 15 as 'one of the places where the spirit of the Council emerges most', draws attention to the fact that the text just quoted places the "accent on the quality of *mystery* of the very being of the *community*. (. . .) The Decree begins by recalling that common life is the actualization of the fraternal *koinonia* of everyone, through the presence of the Lord Jesus in person. From this it concludes that community announces to the world the coming of Christ. The expression of brotherly love, mutual respect, the desire to carry one another's burden, are nothing else than the translation into human acts of the profound, mysterious reality of communion of life with the Father in Jesus, welded together by means of baptism, rooted in the Eucharist, but which all, by their profession, wish to bring to fullness' (*Le grandi leggi del rinnovamento della vita religiosa*, in AA.VV., *Il rinnovamento della vita religiosa*, Florence, 1968, pp.123–128).

10. Conference of Italian Bishops, *La preparazione al sacerdozio ministeriale*, p.111.

11. N. 15, *Enchiridion Vaticanum*, 7, 522.

12. For a deeper treatment I refer the reader to what I have already written: *L'apporto della comunità nel cammino spirituale*, in AA.VV., *La guida spirituale nella vita religiosa*, Rome 1986, pp.123–142. Cf. besides G. Dho, *La formazione del religioso realizzata attraverso la convivenza fraterna e la maturazione della comunità*, in AA VV., *Per una presenza viva dei religiosi nella Chiesa e nel mondo*, Turin 1970, pp. 817–842.

13. C. Lubich, *Diary, 1964–65*, New City Press, New York 1987, p.6.

14. *In Ep. ad Hebr.*, 10, 25, Hom 19, 1.

15. *Longer Rule*, Question 7.

16 *De Mor. Eccl. Cath.*, I, 26, 48.

17. C. Lubich, *L'unità e Gesù Abbandonato*, Rome, 1984, p.104. trans. Why Have You Forsaken Me, New City, London, 1985, p. 98.

18. Th. Matura, *Gospel Radicalism. The Hard Sayings of Jesus*, New York/Dublin 1984, p. 46.

19. C. Lubich, *La vita, un viaggio*, Rome 1984, p. 49.

20. C. Lubich, *In cammino col Risorto*, Rome 1987, pp. 146–147.

EXPERIENCES

Brother Jean Bulteau and the Noviciate of the Brothers of St Gabriel (France)

A chance meeting gives the novices the opportunity to take part in a Mariapolis, one of the summer gatherings of the Focolare Movement, and the life of the noviciate is strengthened by setting the novices on the road of a more practical charity. One of them explained 'it was a decisive stage in my life because it helped me to get straight something I had wanted for some time – a life that was more dedicated to the Lord.'

1 *The meeting with the Focolare Movement July 1964*

As other years, the novices (about 50), went to Boistissandeau, the noviciate house at San-Laurant-Sur-Sevre about 25 kilometres away to allow the brothers of their house to make their retreat. During the journey both the novices and I saw an arrow that we had never seen before with a new word written on it, 'Mariapolis'. We asked each other if it was something to do with the Legion of Mary to which many belong as auxiliary members. The arrows pointed in the direction we were taking and when we came to our destination we realized that our House of St Gabriel was putting up the secretariat of the Mariapolis. A lot of people were coming and going, and a certain number of the participants were being put up in the institute.

As the person in charge of the formation of the novices, I thought it might be a help if they had some contact with this Movement although my only knowledge of it was from its title. So I told the person responsible for the Mariapolis and he arranged it all for us. We took part in two or three of the meetings and then one of the people there, Alain Depreux, came to tell us briefly about the story of the Movement and the principal aspects of its spirituality.

The humility of Alain strongly impressed me and also his deep and peaceful conviction. What struck me personally in the course of the meetings was the fact of the presence of Jesus among those united in his name, (Matthew 18:20) and this was corroborated in the personal experiences following the talks.

This first contact with the Movement led the noviciate into more down to earth charity. Also we had the idea of dividing the novices into groups of five or six for a weekly review of their life and their spiritual formation, and at an attempt at communion with each other.

2. The Mariapolis of 1965 and its effects

But it was above all the Mariapolis of 1965 that enriched the noviciate. As the previous year, and without having planned it beforehand, the dates coincided and we came to San Laurant right at the beginning of the Mariapolis. I asked the novices to take part in the first meeting leaving them then free to follow it or not. In fact they went to almost the whole of it, beginning with Holy Mass in the morning up to the sharing of experiences at the end of the day.

One or two of their descriptions will help to give an idea of the effect that this Mariapolis had on the novices:

These meetings have been for me a source of exceptional grace; they have led to a decisive step in my life in that they have helped me to concentrate strongly on what I have always wanted for some time: a life more committed, more self-giving to the Lord. The numerous and life giving experiences that were shared led me to think that if lay people were able to achieve unity with Christ at this level then there was all the more reason for me, a future religious to do so. I had to sacrifice my selfishness for an exclusive love for him, who is the only object and aim of my life.

I believe I can say that the Lord wanted me to understand better what unity is through the Mariapolis and above all what that brings about: the presence of Jesus among us with all that this implies. So that Jesus may be present I have to love my brother, all my brothers, not with a love that I can feel, but with a supernatural love, seeing Christ in him, and this is now easier for me.

What I liked about the people I met was their evangelical simplicity. I think I quickly guessed their secret, love. He who loves does God's will; if we do God's will we are united.

I learnt then to be united with Jesus suffering and forsaken, and I saw that in this union my own sufferings were easier to bear because I had seen in them what God wills. The thought that Jesus has been forsaken encourages and strengthens me.

3. *The joining of the two noviciates of France (1965)*

Our Superiors decided to bring together the two French noviciates. The chosen place was Boistissandeau. This was August 1965 and there were now more than 60 in the group.

This decision was accepted in faith by both groups but some difficulties ensued. It did seem distressing for those who had to abandon their house and their formation team to come to a completely new place.

Luckily, simplicity triumphed because of the fusion, or rather the unity, of the two groups was achieved quite quickly thanks largely to the welcome which was especially warm for the newly arrived. The spirit of charity had been strengthened at the Mariapolis and so it led to the idea of being at their service in love. Also some little touches won over the newcomers. We tried to give them the best rooms, we tried not to make use of the newly arrived for our benefit, above all we tried not to preach to them but to live well. The result? Quickly the walls of prejudice fell down. The new ones felt welcomed and at home. When they found out about the various groups for sharing, first one and then gradually the others asked if they could take part in them. So by Christmas each of the 14 new arrivals had found a group for themselves. One novice said, 'When I came to Boistissandeau I was not at all happy about it, but from the first month we were made so welcome and we felt such an atmosphere of charity and of brotherly affection, of true unity, that we would have had to have made an effort to turn away from this current of love. What I saw amazed me and I didn't think it was normal, it was too beautiful. So one Sunday I had a conversation two hours long with one of the older brothers who explained these groups to me and, of Jesus in the midst. I realized that it is necessary to love, always to love. From the beginning I accepted everything naturally, as it were in a nutshell, but it is only by living that we truly learn about all this'.

4. *Opening to the Movement*

To safeguard this new vitality and to deepen it we kept ourselves linked to the Movement which we understood had been brought to birth by God to spread the ideal of the Gospel and especially of unity. So some members of the Focolare came from Paris to stay for a weekend in the noviciate. The magazine New City began to be read by the novices together with some copies of *Meditations* written by Chiara Lubich, the foundress of the Movement. At the beginning of December 1965, Alfredo Zirondoli came to give a retreat of three days to the novices, so we learnt the points of the spirituality of the Movement together with the personal witness of Alfredo. But Alfredo was not alone, three members of the Focolare came with him to help to assure, by their unity, the presence of Jesus, who alone gives light and converts. During the meetings they mixed with the novices and their attitude of listening and of service was especially contagious.

And so we continued to take part in the summer meetings of the following years, especially those at Todez. The Superiors gave permission to take part without any difficulty and I attribute a great deal of importance to that. It seemed so useful to me that our young people could be immersed for a few days among God's people who are so diverse and who are living the Gospel day by day. More than the simple and persuasive talks, the experiences that we learnt about were of great value, and they came from such diverse backgrounds.

Time passed, the novices became scholastics and are now spread among different communities. Today the spirit of the Movement is alive in various places belonging to the brothers of St Gabriel and it is also thanks to them that the Movement has been able to spread in Western France and in many missionary zones in Africa and Madagascar.

Fr Irénée Rigolot of the Abbey of Timadeuc (France)

This is the story of an officer of the French Foreign Legion who consecrated his life to God with the enthusiasm of a convert. When he met the spirituality of unity, he discovered unknown dimensions of this consecration 'like rediscovering the privilege of being ourselves; Cistercian monks in the post conciliar Church.' In this Church, where he felt his family was from then on, he wanted to make himself one with God enthusiastically, which is the specific vocation of a contemplative.

I am a Trappist monk and my name is Irénée. For nine years I was an officer in the French Army and while in Algeria often faced death. I fell seriously ill and for a long time was in hospital, and amid those difficulties I felt again that inner call which had come to me when I was twelve, inviting me to the perfect joy of following Jesus. On my bed I decided to give my life completely to God. My health returned and I gave up my rank as a Captain and left everything to become a monk of the Cistercian Trappist Abbey of Timadeuc.

On becoming a monk I believed I had 'truly chosen God' as St Benedict says in his Rule (Chapter 58), with the strong determination of a repentant sinner, and the impulse of a person who has been touched by God's grace: 'You have touched me and my heart is inflamed with love for your peace.' (St Augustine, *Confessions* Chapter 8).

In his merciful goodness the Lord had granted me wonderful graces. He showed himself to me in his tenderness, and the more I met him in prayer, the more I felt the joy of

114

being with him, which encouraged me to look for him even more. I had discovered God through his grace and I was sure of his personal and trinitarian love. At the same time, and it is only now that I am aware of it, I was crucifying him. As far as I was concerned my brothers of the community who welcomed me did not exist truly for me, and my companions in the noviciate suffered a great deal. I had chosen to look for God alone; it seemed to me that I had found him. Of what interest were my brothers to me?

Seeing me fully immersed in my 'contemplation', but at the same time understanding my flight from all that is real, and my difficulties in relating to others, and also afraid for my health, the novice master suggested that I take part in the experience of 'unity' that he was engaged in with two other monks in the light of the spirituality of the Work of Mary (Focolare Movement). After reflecting about this, and reassured by the Marian aspect of the Movement, I accepted 'under obedience'. It was true that I did feel attracted by something new which shone out from that small group; maybe it was their simplicity or their quiet joy, their attention for each person, or their spirit of service. It was not possible to be unaware of all these things and I wanted to know what their secret was.

It was very difficult for me. It meant a real death to myself, a real 'loss of God' to rediscover him in my neighbour. I had to recognize my neighbour in his or her true identity, and make an act of faith that God was there. Later the experience of a fraternal life lived in mutual love, would confirm the fact of that presence of God.

In 1971 there was a change of Abbot. It was still in that period of adaptation after the Vatican Council. There were many difficulties in living unity in brotherly charity. It was then that the new Abbot, judging the tree by its fruits, decided to learn more for himself about this 'Work of Mary'. He heard about the story of the Movement; he read some writings of Chiara Lubich. He shared all of this with the community when he was persuaded of its authenticity; he told us that some of the monks, whom he named, had begun an experience of a life in unity, and from it they had drawn real spiritual profit; and so he thought it was his duty to encourage this experience, and to allow the monks who felt called to it to share in it in all freedom.

From that moment the initial group was opened to anyone who wanted to share in this life of unity. In fact there were two groups, and ten monks took part in them (one quarter of the community). We tried to live the 'Word of Life'[1] sharing with each other once a week the experiences we had had. We tried always to have among us the presence of Jesus, continually renewing our love for each other. This seemed like rediscovering the privilege of being ourselves, Cistercian monks in the Church after the Vatican Council.

While we had lived next to each other up to then, now a convergence of our lives was happening which transformed our relationships with each other as brothers, for the human and spiritual maturing of many of us. In the light of this charism of Chiara, we discovered the charism of our fathers of Citeaux, and the specific emphasis they placed on asceticism for the fulfilment of fraternal charity. The Cistercian life became for us a 'school of charity', a journey together towards the fulfilment of the testament of Jesus 'that they may all be one'. We discovered, in fact, the unifying principle of our religious life: unity in love; and conforming to Jesus crucified, with all the asceticism that implies, is the source of that unity, while the presence of Jesus among us is its marvellous fruit.

Since I have tried to live this new life, my relationships with the others have gradually changed. My life is much more simple. I try to do God's will in everything by giving great importance to each request that comes from my brothers, since in that request I recognize a privileged call of Jesus who invites me to respond to him crucified. He it is in fact that I have chosen to love, preferring him to every other person, Jesus crucified and forsaken is my only good, my only treasure. Constantly referring to him makes me 'a single spirit' with all the members of my community, and this guarantees the presence of Jesus among us insofar as I am responsible for it. I do not have anything else to do than to ensure that this presence is constant; that is what is essential. Now I find I do not have any more time to 'do things', I only find time to cling to God's will in the present moment. We are always 'in debt' as

St Paul says (Rom. 13:8) and never 'entirely free' because the ideal is God's love and it is always possible to love Love.

My relationships with the order have the same kind of stamp. I can 'make myself one' with others, so that Jesus is present among us, when news reaches us of the Cistercian order, or when monks come to stay for a day or two in the Abbey. Since I met the work of Mary, my order has appeared¹ to me more beautiful each day; I love it with all my heart and my joy in being part of it grows, in the proportion that my eyes are opened to the beauty of each of the other religious orders which make up the world of religious life.

I find myself growing more and more a Cistercian-Trappist monk, while the other religious in other orders are increasingly my 'neighbours', truly my brothers. My heart and soul have been enlarged by all that concerns other religious; everything that leads me to have a fuller life has the same effect, and so do the affairs of the entire Church. I sense a greater union with God in all this.

The fact remains that for me, within this huge family, I feel that I am called in a very strong way to incarnate that aspect of the Christian life which is union with God. This is our specific vocation as 'contemplatives' for the benefit of all, in a strict union of heart and soul with everybody.

Gildo Dominici SI

This is the story of Jesus on the cross who cries out: 'My God why have you forsaken me?' in the daily life of a missionary. 'I understood that in the journey towards holiness there are no short cuts; to reach Calvary we must hobble along slowly and with great effort.' It may be loneliness or one's own defects that are so difficult to kill, or the difficulties of being open to others, or being misunderstood and rejected that is the problem. The important thing is 'to live Jesus forsaken in the details of life doing God's will in the present moment'.

From 1976 to 1977 I went to the formation school, which is

now at Loppiano, near Florence, Italy. The school is for those men in religious orders who want to deepen their knowledge of the spirituality of the Work of Mary. When the school had finished, my heart and soul were full of God. As I walked along the roads in Rome or through the streets in Indonesia, I was able to see God everywhere; I used to adore him in every person I met. It was all so beautiful; I was living in a state of reconciliation with God, with myself and with the world. The fact is that the school had been for me as Mount Tabor was for the Apostles; seven months of wonderful light, of intense mutual love which had made each of us transparent for the other.

Only ten days after the school was over, I left for Indonesia and quite soon I was in the desert. It was an unknown country, utterly different to Vietnam where I had been for seven years. Worst of all it was a place where there was nobody with whom I could share this spirit of unity. I felt completely alone in a 'strange' land. In a few days I had passed from the light and warmth of 'Jesus in the midst' to the North Pole of loneliness; Jesus on the cross forsaken. I immediately embraced him; I told him I was ready to remain in Indonesia for all my life if necessary, if this was his will.

Quite soon I met an even greater difficulty than loneliness. Little by little I realized that the seven months in the school had indeed been full of shining light, but it was a light that had remained outside the spirit. This ideal that I had learnt had not really deeply affected me. After a few months I was the same as I had always been, with the same defects, with the same 'old man'. I believed that I had been reborn, but instead I found myself unchanged.

Undoubtedly I was deeply disillusioned. I realized then that in the journey towards holiness there are no short cuts. There is no way of avoiding Calvary and you cannot fly over it in a jet plane; it is necessary to hobble up it slowly and with great effort. In all this sense of failure, embracing 'Jesus forsaken' gave me strength to live those years with intensity. Remembering that Jesus in the Eucharist meant a great deal to me, I visited him often and was strongly united with him. I tried to love my brothers in religious life, and I did bring a new atmosphere into the community as the Provincial told me in a letter. In those two years, my ideal of unity found solid support from the other religious whom I had known during the school. They did not write to me often, but their letters were very full and I used to read and re-read them continually. This was the first stage of my 'noviciate with Jesus forsaken'.

The second stage began in the August of 1979 when I was sent to work full time with the Vietnamese refugees. Those were years of hard and intense work, decisive years in my life, years of the desert, of a school of life with 'Jesus forsaken'. I decided to give my all to my brother refugees, to love them along four basic ways.

Firstly, to make myself one with them by accepting them, choosing to live in their midst, sharing their life fully, including their difficulties. I wanted to be a presence of love among them just as Jesus is in the Eucharist. I still remember that Autumn day in 1979 when I returned after visiting a camp on a faraway island in the China Sea. I had been away one month. We lived in straw huts and my little room was next to the hut which served as a church. The tabernacle was half in the church and half in my room. Going into the room, genuflecting, a thought struck me; I had been away, but he had remained among the refugees, a presence of love. I wanted to be like him.

Secondly, as a practical expression of love, I would arrange an intense programme of social assistance. The refugee is a person who has lost everything, is wounded in his spirit and has been uprooted culturally and socially. In journeying towards a social and cultural environment which is not his own, he needs help, love and respect. My openness and understanding has increased year by year. For example, at the beginning I established a special time for welcoming people, but afterwards I abandoned that to be at the disposition of Jesus in every brother, whatever the hour.

Thirdly, I tried to share the spirit of unity with the refugees. All my apostolic effort was directed in forming a loving community, especially among the young people, inspired by the Gospel, which we tried to live together word by word. Many interesting experiences from a shared life were born from this. For example, one day I lost my patience and shouted harshly at a lady; it was towards evening. The following morning I went to celebrate Mass and when I reached the altar, I realized that the woman was there in church. Jesus explains that without previous reconciliation the Mass has no value, so after I had asked God for forgiveness for our sins, publicly I asked forgiveness from that woman for my lack of love the previous day. Then there was Hanh, a young Vietnamese girl who had lost six of her family who died of thirst during the sea voyage. She had accused the owner of the boat, a Buddhist, of denying a little bit of drinking water to her loved ones. The result: hatred between the two families. But after three months of life in the camp, in that climate of love in the Christian community, she herself came spontaneously to ask me to reconcile her with the Buddhist family. We did so publicly during a Mass; this made an enormous impression on the whole camp.

Finally, in those years I fully realized the effort needed for loving. Loving is beautiful, but it asks a heavy price. Loving demands a continuous effort, dying to oneself. I discovered that in between my desire to love and loving effectively, there was in the middle my hard, difficult, and rather leathery personality. Loving according to the Gospel is extremely difficult for me. Each day I have to begin again the hard battle to soften, and make my character more gentle and sweet. During the meditation in the morning I tell Jesus that I am ready to love, to see him and love him in each refugee, but five minutes later I am impatient and hard with the first person that I meet. This is my daily effort.

These four aspects of my love are, on the other hand, 'faces of Jesus forsaken.' To share the life of the refugees, to be always at their disposition, never to have five minutes for oneself and to accept oneself, an unloving person, is hard; it is to be like Jesus forsaken on the cross. But it is by means of this day-to-day struggle, that the spirituality of the Focolare penetrates within and is born in myself. It is by means of this daily effort that little by little love is entering within me.

Too slowly, perhaps, so in my third stage Jesus all of a sudden put his foot down on the accelerator. I left Indonesia and I came to the Philippines in May of 1985, surrounded by the aura of success, of being an 'expert' in work among refugees. But Jesus had a lesson in reserve. I myself knew that my life was not nearly intense enough, that my heart had not been wholly for God. So during the month of December 1985, my prayer practically consisted in repeating a single phrase: 'Jesus touch my heart' referring to the woman of the gospel who was healed from her flow of blood by simply touching the clothes of Jesus.

Jesus began to listen to me in a way that I would never have imagined. In January of 1986, there was a misunderstanding with a person for whom I felt some attachment. This led me to understand the inconsistency of a love that is not supernatural. In April I received a threatening letter in which there were three bullets. Either leave the camp or be killed! In September, coming back from America and with a new administration running the camp, there was another humiliation. I no longer received permission to go back into the camp; I had to wait at its gate for two whole months.

In contrast to Indonesia it had been a failure, a 'losing' in the Gospel sense. In Indonesia I was 'rich' in my programmes, in my results, rich with prestige among the International Agencies for my influence and authority over the refugees. In the Philippines instead, the Lord had made me 'poor'. My plans had been thrown out, my very person rejected, thrown out from the International Agencies, completely thrown out from the camp, until I had to abandon everything and go away.

The temptation was to ask why, but I remembered Jesus too on the cross had asked why without receiving any reply. 'My God, my God why have you forsaken me?' No! I do not want to have any answer, I do not want to analyse it all, I want only to embrace Jesus forsaken, 'always, immediately and joyfully'. I know that everything is love. Jesus is leading me on the road of being stripped of everything. I remember a sentence that I read in *Idipsum Sentientes*, the little news letter which links the religious who have been at the school in Loppiano, 'when you are truly nothing, then you will fulfil the great things which you have always wanted to do.' The greatest thing I have wanted is to become capable of loving;

it is the road of Jesus forsaken. Now I am in the third stage, living Jesus forsaken in the details of my life, doing his will in the present moment.

REFERENCES
1. A sentence from scripture that members of the Focolare Movement try to put into practice month by month.

IV CONTRIBUTIONS TOWARDS THE INTEGRATED FORMATION OF THE PERSON

Many in one Body

Fr Bonaventure Marinelli OFM

1. 'God so loved the world that he gave his only Son' (John 3:16) 'so that we might live through him' (1 John 4:9). We have all received the one Spirit and we have been clothed with the one Christ. We may be compared to consecrated hosts: individually each one is Christ, and collectively they are still the one Christ, even though there are many hosts and they may be in different places.

On the day of Pentecost the Holy Spirit appeared as tongues of fire over the heads of each of the 120 disciples present in the upper room (Acts 2:3). But the disciples did not then go about, each with his own little flame over his head, each with his own little piece of the Holy Spirit. The Holy Spirit cannot be carved into little pieces. When he comes upon people, he inserts each one into Christ, like shoots on a single vine. He preserves the individuality of each person, but he also introduces among them something which binds them together in a deep living relationship. They are like members of a single living organism: although they are many, although they are different, they form together one single body: the Body of Christ (1 Cor. 12:27), the whole Christ.

2. This mystery of our unity in the one Christ is what constitutes God's loving plan for humankind, and it gives therefore the final meaning of the life, death, and resurrection of Christ. 'It is better for one man to die . . . to gather together in unity the scattered children of God' (John 11: 47–52). Jesus did not die and rise from the dead simply so that each person

should save his own soul, but 'to gather together in unity the scattered children of God'. In his priestly prayer, he said: Father, 'the glory (i.e. the divine life) which thou hast given me I have given to them, that they may be one even as we are one' (John 17:22). Jesus received divine life from the Father (incarnation) and shared it with human beings (life, death, and resurrection). He did this not so that each one should be made holy for his own sake but 'that they may be one'.

This was God's intention for humanity which Jesus came to restore. Particularly informative in this respect is the biblical account of the tower of Babel (Gen. 11: 1–9). After the fall, human beings multiplied upon the earth, but gradually divisions sprang up: people against people, race against race, family against family, individual against individual. The people of the plain of Shinar observed this disastrous process of division. They said: 'Let us build a tower ... so that we may not be scattered about the whole earth' – *ne dividamur super terram*. In other words, so that we do not continue to divide and fight each other, let us organize ourselves in a unity that is political, administrative, economic, and religious. And they planned this, not against God but leaving God out of the picture. The result? A division worse than before. This is a story that has been repeated so often. Every time an empire has risen, it has hoped to eliminate war and division once and for all. And every time it has all resulted in divisions even worse than before. This was the case in ancient times with the Assyrian, Babylonian, Egyptian and Roman empires, and in our own time, with the League of Nations. And let us not fool ourselves: the United Nations will be the same if it does not base its efforts on Christ. Because only God can rebuild the unity that man has destroyed. It is only in Christ that humanity can rediscover its meeting point, its principle of unity.

3. Salvation history is precisely this: the history of the rebuilding of humankind's unity in Christ. People of God, Body of Christ, the whole Christ: these terms hide a mysterious reality about which God speaks to us only in images suited to direct our instinct of faith. We find the principles listed in the first chapter of Lumen Gentium. Let us highlight the

most significant. The *edifice*: it is not a pile of bricks thrown in one spot, but bricks built on one another so that each is held up by the others and helps to keep the others in place. Each contributes to the stability and beauty of the whole lot, and each brick accepts hiding at least three of its faces for the sake of the building. The *people* of God, the *kingdom* of God: not a chaotic horde, but persons who belong to the same race, to the same culture, who speak the same language, live under the same laws, are involved in the same events, both favourable and unfavourable. The *vine*: through the trunk each shoot is united to all the others and with them forms one vine. Each shoot lives its life in common with the rest: it circulates either life-giving enzymes or deadly poisons which affect the rest of the plant, contributing therefore either positively or negatively to the life and fruitfulness of the whole. Finally, the *Body* (1 Cor. 12:12): a feature of the body is the multiplicity and diversity of its limbs, organs, and functions. But in the midst of all this diversity and multiplicity, there is a profound togetherness which unites and co-ordinates everything, so that no cell lives for itself alone, but for the whole organism.

These images guide the perception of our faith. But they would also direct our commitment to formation and life. In our personal behaviour and reciprocal relationships we must give expression to this profound, mysterious reality: that, although we are many and diverse, we are the one Body of Christ.

4. This mystery, hidden through the ages, was manifested in Christ, and it is coming to the fore in Christian awareness particularly in our time. In the documents of the First Vatican Council no reference is made to the Church as the Body of Christ, but Leo XIII spoke of it some years later in the encyclical *Divinum Illud*. Pius X drew attention to it in his encyclical on our Blessed Lady, and Pius XI in his encyclical on the Sacred Heart. In 1943 Pius XII made it the explicit subject of his encyclical *Mystici Corporis*, in the introduction to which he said that this mystery of the Body of Christ is precisely what is coming to the forefront of Christian awareness in our times, and will have a great

influence in the future. Finally, Vatican II in *Lumen Gentium* presents the Church to us in its mysterious reality as People of God, Body of Christ, the whole Christ. The other Council documents are like fifteen beams of light bathing the various aspects of Christian living in modern times in the light of this mystery. Since Vatican II this mystery has tended to become the central thesis of theology. In preaching and conferences it is being referred to more and more.

5. The love of God, however, did not reveal his plan for humankind and involve us in it merely for us to construct theologies and make it the object of preaching and conferences. No! We have to translate it into the everyday reality of our personal and social lives. The mystery of Christ's body, commits us to a process of self-formation which makes us move from the individualistic spirituality, in which we have been trained, to a spirituality based on the Mystical Body. This is a difficult step to take, a bit like crossing the Red Sea to enter the promised land.

So what does such a change mean? What does it entail? First of all, we must recognize this: that although Jesus began his preaching saying, 'You must therefore be perfect as your heavenly Father is perfect' (Matt. 5:48), at the end of his three years of teaching he said something very different. In his priestly prayer, when he summed up his teaching, he did not say, 'Father, I pray that they may be perfect as you are perfect'; instead, he said: 'Father, that they may become perfectly one' (John 17:23). Recognizing this means grasping immediately the fundamental importance of reciprocal love: *Ante omnia mutuam charitatem habentes* ('Above all hold unfailing your love for one another'). Above all: before all else: before recreation, before work, before the apostolate, even before prayer and the Mass.

This new outlook involves a shift in the direction of spiritual effort: from tending towards perfection and holiness for oneself to a commitment 'to become holy together'. Certainly I will continue in the ascetic struggle to rid myself of my faults and acquire virtue, particularly the virtue of charity, but I will no longer do this for my own perfection so much as out of love for my brothers and sisters: *Pro eis sanctifico me ipsum*

126

'For their sake I dedicate myself to you' (John. 17:19). In other words, I will strive to better myself, but not for my own sake, not even for my own holiness; no! for the unity of the brethren. I will struggle to eliminate whatever causes division, to facilitate whatever unites, so that I encourage around me the building of better relationships, genuine participation and collaboration, an ever greater readiness to lay down our lives for one another. In this way, Jesus' promise will be expressed in reality: 'Where two or three are gathered in my name, there am I in the midst of them' (Matt. 18:20). This is what really matters, not my sanctity. In this case I will be made holy, as a bonus!

Passing from an individualistic spirituality to a spirituality of the Mystical Body also means that we must train ourselves to a lively sense of responsibility in every situation in life. 'None of us lives for himself only' (Rom. 14:7). My behaviour, even my most personal and private behaviour, affects the whole Mystical Body either positively or negatively. Mine is a light, and grace, and life, that is either kindled and burns, or else weakens and dies out, in some part of the Mystical Body.

A spirituality based on the Mystical Body means developing an awareness that my health, my intelligence, my abilities, my time, my goods, are not simply my property. They are goods which I hold and administer for the benefit of the family of God. Consequently, I must make myself ever more aware that I do not study simply for the sake of my own personal stock of learning; I do not take rest simply for the sake of my own health; I do not work simply to express my own needs and sense of value; I do not pray simply to cultivate my own spiritual life; I do not undergo suffering only for the sake of my own holiness, but 'in my flesh I complete what is lacking in Christ's afflictions (life and death) for the sake of his body, that is, the Church' (Col. 1:24).

Such a spirituality will also mean that I grasp more clearly that I can and must give expression to this reality of the Mystical Body in every aspect of life. Therefore I will recognize the strength I have as a member of the Body of Christ. When I clench my fist, I do so not only with the strength in the muscles of my fingers: I use the power of my brain, heart, liver, my whole body. When God's will entrusts me with some task, I must not feel that I bear it alone, that I have only my own poor ability; I must remember that behind me I have the strength of the whole Mystical Body, the power of Jesus present in the disciples united in his name. I may feel inadequate, powerless, but I must remember that God chooses (and uses) what is weak in the world to shame the strong (1 Cor. 1:27). If Samson could do marvels with the jawbone of an ass, what can Jesus in our midst not do with a complete ass?

6. It is not for our own benefit that we are religious. We are religious for the sake of the people of God. We have to form ourselves so as to contribute to the formation of the people of God. We have to exert ourselves, both personally and communally, to move from an individualistic spirituality to a spirituality of the Mystical Body, so that we can help the people of God to take the same step. And we must do this by our presence and life style rather than by our preaching and apostolic activity. Gradually, as we develop within ourselves and within our communities a real life of unity, we will glow with this life and, even without knowing it, we will be the yeast of a culture and spirituality of the Mystical Body in our environment.

7. We are surrounded by fearful problems, greater than our strength: global problems such as atheism, hunger, drugs, and so forth. But there are also the seemingly simpler problems such as the renewal of our institutes, formation, vocations, etc. A saint could not solve them, not even a whole squadron of saints! Only Jesus, the Holy One *par excellence*, can do it. He always has the ability to attract hearts, he always remains the pre-eminent master and teacher, who can guarantee a true formation of young people and a renewal of institutes which is more than a mere facelift. God is always the Almighty One, who can melt atheism like snow before the sun, and solve all other problems with a word. But he can do this only if we give him the chance, making him present, powerfully present.

Yet here is a problem, greater than anything already mentioned. We cannot drag Jesus down from heaven! No – he has already descended, he is already in our midst. He is present, and we are his Body. However, his presence remains, so to speak, inactive, dormant, until we make an effort to give concrete expression to it. We have to behave as his Body, as members of his Body. Jesus is present, but his presence is unproductive because, in practice, we give expression to ourselves, not to him. Each of us walks by himself, guided for the most part by programmes and structures, by the spirit of discipline and a general sense of collaboration. We do not walk as living members of his Body. Jesus was present in the boat on the lake during the storm. He slept. No – it's not that he slept. The Apostles slept, and when they woke up and took notice of his presence, he had no difficulty sorting out the problem.

Every religious community is called to be a presence of Jesus, that is, of Jesus wide awake, a small Mystical Body of his. The brothers must therefore remain alert too, conscious of the presence of Jesus (among them). This presence is always to be lived, to be strengthened, in a unity that is ever more concrete and shared in. It is to be expressed in the various undertakings and activities of the community, which are lived precisely as an expression of the presence of Jesus rather than as an expression of the personalities and abilities of the members. In the final analysis, this is what is intended by the periodic community gatherings provided for in the constitution of all institutes.

It is only in this way that our communities will regain their full meaning in our changing world. It is not enough that they are communities of holy people who live side by side, even if they do not damage each other's haloes like rams cracking each other's horns. They must make present the Holy One *par excellence*, so that it is he who shines through the life and activity of the individual members.

8. Certainly, this is a demanding task which can easily be forgotten. But even here Jesus comes to meet us in a sacrament: the *Eucharist*. The Eucharist is the sacrament of our life in Christ. It is also the sacrament of our unity in him,

of our being his Body. Through the sacramental signs, Jesus says to me: 'I am your life: live me.' He also says, 'I am the life of your brothers and sisters: see me and love me in them.' Indeed, 'You are not so many Christs: you are my Body; be my Body, my visible, active presence!'

When he was instructing the new communicants, St John Chrysostom once asked: 'What is on the altar?' And then after Communion he asked them: 'What have you received?' They answered: 'Christ.' 'What have you become?' 'Christ.' He insisted: 'Many Christs or only one?' They replied: 'Only one!'

St Augustine reminds us that the eucharistic bread is not made from a single grain, but from many grains ground together, kneaded together, baked together. This fact speaks to us about unity. In order for the words of consecration to make Jesus present, it is not enough that they are said over a pile of grains, even if these are the best, the choicest. For the community to be the Body of Christ, it is not enough that the members are upright and holy: they must be ground, kneaded, and baked together, with all that these images suggest.

Our faith in the Eucharist will remain incomplete if we do not translate it into a concrete effort to live, singly and together, what the Eucharist tells us we are. It will be incomplete if we do not seek to do our part so that the little Body of Christ, which is our community, is really a 'body' – a well-tuned body, in which every member and part fulfils its function in a living harmony with the others. We must not give the painful impression of suffering from partial paralysis: having one eye directed upwards, the other looking down; one useless arm and the other out of control; one lame foot and the other shuffling along.

9. Mary is Mother of the Church, and our mother therefore, insofar as we form the Body of Christ: may she draw us into a closer unity around her, like the 120 disciples waiting for the first Pentecost in the upper room; so that the Holy Spirit may bring about the presence of Jesus in our midst in a way that is more vivid and more effective.   Amen.

Contributions towards the Integrated Formation of the Person

Fr. Amedeo Ferrari OFM Conv.

Introduction

We are all conscious that in the times in which we live the breath of the Holy Spirit is particularly active. Also we are immersed in the flux of renewal, which Vatican II has brought into the various fields of religious life, not least into education and formation.

A lot of research has been done, in-depth studies have been made using all human and religious science, from anthropology to sociology, from psychology to theology, from philosophy to psychiatry and 'prossemics'.[1]

All these studies on humanity, especially in regard to the formation of the person, point to a clearly felt desire to reach a more all-embracing and deeper concept which will give meaning to all that a human being is, in all the aspects of his make-up.

Grasping the significance of a concept is neither easy to achieve, nor is it something we are used to doing, especially in regard to humanity. Yet it is necessary for a discussion on formation.

Take nature around us. The scent of a flower which delights our senses opens up for us a whole vista. The earth has drunk in the rain; its colour is the condensation of the atmosphere and the seasons; its sap is fed from the *humus* of the earth into which all human refuse goes. The entire universe, in fact, is working together in each event as if the flower's destiny is to lead on to something else, to the person who appreciates it.

The whole universe is tending towards humanity, expecting to be understood by human feelings and then interpreted by the human spirit, by the interior dimension of humankind, where it finds its meaning. The spirit brings together the entire wealth of the universe as in a mirror, discovering the harmony of unity in learning the significance of each part. Who then can make sense of the yearning in the human heart to be a person?

Meaning for Humanity

Suppose an artist wants to create a masterpiece. He must have an inspiration which comes to fruition in his heart and mind that gives the work of art its sense and meaning. What is the inspiration that makes sense of being human? Every man and woman, whoever they are, feels deeply the need to discover who can explain the fact that they are a person. Pope John Paul II has no doubts. 'The one who wishes to understand himself thoroughly . . . must draw near to Christ',[2] because 'Christ makes his supreme calling clear'.[3]

This knowledge is communion

To find out our real vocation is to discover the source of our life, and then, remaining always in contact with the life-giving source, we can reach our fulfilment.[4] This cannot be achieved by reading books and articles, or in learned research and study. This knowledge and contact with what is life-giving can only come through a living experience, by communion with this source of life, by participating in it. 'To understand man in his unity and especially in his relationship with God' writes Fr. Foresi, 'rationalization, judgements and syllogisms are inadequate'.[5] We must have a knowledge based on love, on a relationship that touches the intimate and most anciently recognized structures of life, what Pascal calls 'the heart'.

132

It is love that is the origin of this knowledge. A person responsible for formation, gifted in this love, is able to enter that 'sanctum' where the divine artist is at work, completing his loving activity. It is the Holy Spirit who establishes the unique and irrepeatable being of each person.

It is said of Thomas Aquinas that at the end of his life he gave up writing. His secretary complained that his work was incomplete and it ought to be finished. Thomas replied: 'While I was celebrating Mass a few months ago I felt God's presence. I have had no desire to do any more writing from then on. In fact, I think all I've written about God has no value'.[6] For the Christian, knowledge is transformed by what is known in love. This experience, a living thing, is the basis for the formation of the 'new man' as Paul has it in his epistles.

The tensions from being in the world

According to psychoanalysis, the baby's first feeling on opening his eyes on this world, is of fear and distress. It is the tender warmth of motherly love that slowly allows this feeling to be replaced by the assurance that growth and development are possible.

Probably the 'new person' has a similar experience when he or she becomes aware of having a seed in their heart, which contains the beginnings of the new life of grace, while at the same time they must go on living in a human society contaminated by sin. Tensions can make them feel pulled apart.

Modern culture cannot but seem more and more eccentric because humanity has lost its centre. This affects people both at a social level and individually. It also affects all that is sacred, including those in religious life. The Christian and the religious live in the world while not being of the world and all the conflicts and wounds of society affect them.

Let us underline briefly three areas of tension that can compromise the harmonious growth into maturity of the religious in their daily life.

a. They may be used to an individualistic outlook on life and have an idealized view of perfection. What they feel they ought to be is not linked to daily experience which can consist in mistakes, failures and falls, all of which they reject within themselves. This could lead to an unconscious rejection of oneself, to an alienation so to speak from life. For instance, the religious may talk of the ideal of justice – and it is a noble truth – but they may not be just to the person with whom they are living. Or they may proclaim the virtue of poverty without being poor themselves, because they are attached to their own way of looking at things and their own ideas. Or they may preach a lot about God without having had the chance to experience him as love.

b. A second tension arises because of the desire to be an important personality, and to have and possess. We are formed to think that fulfilment means affirming oneself over others, having our own ideas, being admired, being able to cope with any situation. The ego, with all its needs, becomes the hub around which all revolves to the detriment of the needs of the community, of its work and structures. Our consumer society favours the desire to have since we think the fulfilled person is the one who possesses knowledge, university degrees, esteem, affection and power. We think the same in the spiritual field. Even the relationship with God can be transformed into a desire to possess; and if we feel we no longer possess him, we doubt his love. So the ego wants to feel secure, but finds itself with an empty heart and feels dead.

c. Another strong tension we experience is between 'being' and 'doing', between being and the function we perform. Our consumer society values producing and consuming, the person is of value for what they do, a person is identified with the function they perform. Jung confirms this when he states, 'The modern individual is reduced to the rank of a simple functionary, since this alone has any collective value and consequently can give him any sense of value in his life'.[7] But this precisely causes the problem and leads to a nervous breakdown. A religious was telling me how difficult it was to pull together all the tasks entrusted to him; youth chaplain in school, organizing his studies, prayer, recreation, completing his theology, youth activities at the weekend in a parish. He was about to suffer a nervous breakdown which would mean a long illness. Many a religious, especially the ordained priest is tempted to fall into the activity trap, to be in a role more linked, with social activity than with his or her true being.

The 'new person' feels all these diverse pulls of the world and realizes the need to overcome the tensions. 'New persons' know they have the seed of a new life within, but they do not have the formation to overcome the problem. If they had, then they would be free from any conditioning by the situation around them, and they could reach their maturity and fulfilment.

The 'new person' is always coming to birth

Formation has many different aspects and one of them is emphasized by the etymology of the word 'educate'. It comes from the Latin, 'educere', to bring out into the light what already exists yet is hidden, and to promote development once in the light.

For the human being, all that constitutes the 'new person' must be brought out and then an integrated formation will be achieved. 'The Father has projected his own perfect image in the Son, and Jesus is the first born amongst many brothers' says St. Paul.[8] He is the image to which all are predestined to conform.

In trying to conform to Jesus, one of the first things to strike us might be his ability to live out all the tensions that face a person without becoming their victim. Jesus of Nazareth seems to have overcome all tensions, and in conforming to him, a person is called to do the same. Jesus is fully God: 'He who sees me has seen the Father', but also fully human. As Pope John Paul II has said: 'He laboured with human hands, he thought with a human mind, he loved with a human heart'.[9] Three astonishing though essential elements belong to our conformity in Christ; the vocation to love, the image of the Trinity in us, the incarnation of his love – himself in us.

The vocation to love

It is in the Jesus-image that we discover the first element that constitutes us a 'new person', and this is what qualifies us to stand before God in an 'I-Thou' relationship: i.e. A person can have with God/love a relationship of knowledge, love, communion and friendship.

This relationship with God is not something 'added on' or 'extra' to the quality of being human, just another quality of humanity. It is essential for being a person, for being human. It is precisely because of the spiritual aspect in humanity that a person is able to be open to the other. The Pope underlines this: 'God writes in to the humanity of both man and woman the vocation for loving, and so the capability and responsibility for love and communion.'[10] Every aspect of humanity is included: 'Love embraces also the human body; the body shares in this spiritual love'.[11]

Now to set in motion this quality and to correspond to it by living in a loving way, the 'new person' needs to be attracted by the care and attention of Somebody.

For a baby, the most important influence in its first few months of life, is not so much the physical surroundings of its home, its brothers and sisters and so on, as the loving care of its mother. So every 'new person' to live in the supernatural, needs to feel they were born out of love from Someone who has loved them first and foremost, and continues to love them. 'I exist in so far as I am loved. To exist implies having an experience of being thought about, remembered and known by God.'[12] Our development as an individual is linked to this first act of loving welcome; and not to accept this is to reject the whole process of being what we are meant to be; as if a photographic negative rejected the light.

136

When love's ray caresses the soul, there is the possibility of a free and personal radical response; the choice of that love alone as a worthwhile ideal for life. Love is the aim and the motive force of the 'new person' in all life's details. Each day can be consecrated to love. We need always to begin again and again and again to love. Beginning again to live each day according to the will of God, Love breaks the monotony of life and prevents us being stuck in a particular groove, or being fossilized by our habits, good though they may be. Beginning again teaches the 'new person' to live in the time of Love, which is the time of God, the present moment. Fenelon called the present moment 'a little eternity'.

By this choice and way of living the 'new person' feels an interior unity in a process of divinization which St Maximus explains 'Is the reunification by means of love of created nature with uncreated nature',[13] that is, the creature with the divinity. As in Jesus humanity and divinity are one, so in any person the divine and the human are to be fused into one.'[14]

This leads to the new realization of what a person ought to be, 'God by participation'. The dialectic or tension between what a person should be (the ideal) and what they actually are (the reality) is thus overcome through loving, or love. They discover they must become what they already are at the deepest level, a child of God. Gradually as the divine is allowed to penetrate all levels of the personality, a person's conscience feels it masters and possesses all their faculties and can direct them to build up their unity, by self-giving. Self-giving to God and to one's fellows provides the oxygen for growth in all its dimensions, the sense and purpose of life come back into focus, full maturity can be achieved, because of the continual pull to go beyond self.

The person, image of the Trinity

One's process of divinization is none other than a deepening of the roots of one's own maturing as a human being, as a

137

person. The botanists tell us that the branches of a tree spread out according to the breadth and depth of its roots. Hence, the 'new person', while discovering God within, becomes more and more open to others, and to the measure of their love and self-giving, their unity with God grows, as the tree grows in both root and branches together.

Our formation is dependent on these interpersonal relationships, the second element, which must be a part of our formation, and which must be developed so that men and women may fulfil themselves as persons. A modern and well respected Italian theologian, Bruno Forte writes: 'The divine image of man reflects the Father, Son and Holy Spirit'.[15] An acorn cannot find its true fulfilment without being an oak, obeying the law written in to its being, so the human being, recreated in Jesus to his image, is to come to maturity in a trinitarian way; by becoming a person human beings live in the likeness of the three Persons.

The person fulfilled in the we

We are all well aware that in present day culture there is a specific orientation to emphasize humanity's social aspect; there is a shift from the single to the collective, from the individual to 'intersubjectivity'.

Psychology, sociology, philosophy, anthropology are increasingly aware of the fact that the human being is essentially in relation to others: that 'I' of its very nature implies a relation to 'you'; that 'being with', 'being amongst', and 'living for' are not accidental dimensions, merely skin-deep, but a constitutive element of the person. Some authors go so far as to say that interpersonal relationships are like oxygen for the organism, are the law for the psychological development of the person without which a human being becomes empty and hardened.[16] It is the experience of a relationship with others, of the 'we' which enables a person to find their own centre and fulfil themselves as a person. Mounier, an exponent of Christian personalism, comparing human life to the disciples' journey from Jerusalem to Emmaus, defines it as a journey made 'to the presence of the Person amongst persons'.[17] This directly implies a spiritual experience.

In today's Church there is a flowering of spiritualities that emphasize the communitarian aspect of the Christian life, and among them is the Focolare Movement with its spirituality of unity. 'We go to God by passing through our brothers and sisters', writes Chiara Lubich. 'In fact we go to God together with our brothers and sisters'.[18]

When we are taken up into and possessed by the person of Christ, which is the height of this experience, we discover that instead of being individuals we become a community, and our community becomes ever more 'Church'; and between these Churches grows communion in the Spirit, so the body of the human race has the leaven within it to grow into the Body of Christ. 'The "we" of humanity is built up in this way', writes J Galot.[19]

Formation in relationships

All this could remain purely theoretical and will fail to enter our lives as 'new persons' unless we learn the process of dialogue and of relationships with others.

Natural and supernatural relationships are similar in that the essentials are the same: the 'other', 'me' and our 'relationship'. For a Christian we know that the 'other' is Jesus himself, and we want the 'me' to decrease and the 'other' to increase. But the novelty for the Christian is the third element, the 'relationship', love, which makes possible both giving and receiving.

For the 'new person', the new capability of loving is because of the power of God through the Holy Spirit with whom the person is impregnated. So Christians cannot forget that the love with which they love their neighbour comes from on high; and they have the ability to love insofar as it is God himself acting in the one who loves. Charity alone allows love to be disinterested, to go beyond the limitations of our neighbour's humanity, to love every person without leaving out anybody. In a word, with God, Love is truly human ('I will give you a heart of flesh').

Charity has the ability to create the necessary conditions for authentic relationships: knowing how to be nothing oneself in order to welcome and receive the other person. Between two persons full of their own joys, difficulties and experiences, neither communication nor dialogue can exist if both do not share with each other, receiving and giving. Only the emptying of self permits the other to enter fully into us. In this temple which is our neighbour, we are able to encounter God. Only at art school can we learn the mysteries of art. Only in a school of life do we learn the finer points in the art of loving, of building true relationships in the Spirit. We have as our aim the new commandment of Jesus, 'Love one another as I have loved you', to the utmost limit that the little word 'as' fully intends, which is to the greatest extreme.

Everything takes on meaning as long as we give it away, and although it is an effort we should always try to give everything. For instance the gift of priesthood which a religious may enjoy, or the religious life itself, or the gift of one's own spirituality can all be lived out well if we 'give them away' so to speak, and do not cling to them so that the Christian life itself is obscured. 'Give, and there will be gifts for you'. Concord in a community is so very helpful and can be achieved when the reason for our communion is Jesus himself. Origen affirms that this concord 'contains the Son of God'.[20] Is not this the reason we have left everything and gone to live in a religious community?

It is this communitarian experience of the person of Jesus which fulfils the individual, allowing him or her to become a person. Even our sexuality becomes more manageable when there is the true gift of self in our interpersonal relationships bound up in God's love. John Paul II underlines this: 'The education in love as a gift of self is the indispensable premise for the formation of the person . . . ', and sexuality, if it is directed to interpersonal dialogue, contributes to the integrated maturing of our whole being 'body, emotions and soul, and it manifests its inmost meaning by leading

140

the person to the gift of self in love.'[21] The tension between being and having is thus overcome because the person is totally devoted to being a gift to others.

The paradoxical law in relationships

'He who loses his life will find it'.[22] Experience of this hidden and paradoxical law at the heart of love is when formation in relationships achieves its high point. Love grows the more it is given away; the more we grow less, the more development there is. Modern humanistic psychology confirms that it is necessary 'to lose the false ego in order to find your true personality'.[23] Dostoevsky wrote in his notebook, 'people can fulfil themselves only by not exalting themselves.'[24]

Yet the ego instinctively wants to possess for itself, wants to take over, so how can it take on board this law for its own maturing? Only one model can help and it is not available on the level of intellect, but only on that of life. It is the person of Jesus who on the cross reached the highest expression of self-giving when he cried out, 'My God, my God, why have you forsaken me?' He lost himself completely in that cry: 'Exinanivit seipsum'. When he became nothing it expressed the greatest possibility of that love which achieves unity.

Divine love alone, love which is ours from the crucifixion, explains to us it is by losing ourselves we become ourselves, by giving ourselves completely we lose ourselves, and become in every aspect the person we are meant to be. The ego must die, or rather be dead, to live for the other. On this death grows new life, love, the risen Jesus. The mystery of death and resurrection becomes a daily experience of the relationship between Christians, and this leads us to live with each other in the pattern of the Holy Trinity and brings a person to fulfilment in Jesus.[25]

141

The incarnation of love

The third element for integrated personal formation to be complete, for the 'new person' to conform to Jesus, is that supernatural love has to become incarnate. In the Gospel which is spirit and life we find every aspect of human life impregnated with the divine because God lived as a human being on this earth. If a person learns how to translate the Gospel into every experience of life, then a wonderful discovery is made: that at the heart of all the words of the Gospel, love is to be found. The heart of the one who feeds on the Gospel becomes filled with God, with supernatural love. If their being becomes love in the gift of self to their brothers and sisters, love becomes life in all they do, in all their activities, and so the whole of human existence is transformed into the divine and is an expression of love.

This is what sets the 'new person' at peace and harmony with all creation around them and, furthermore, gives a solution to the agonizing problem of the work ethic. Whether we study, or are at work, at rest, with our family, in school, involved in politics, doing pastoral work, confined to bed or jogging to keep fit, all are expressions of different aspects of the life of the 'new person', love. Jesus begins to live and grow in each of us in age, wisdom and grace as happened to him in Nazareth, and we experience the powerful revolution brought by him to this world. Christian formation really means that instead of our ego, Jesus, or supernatural love is let live in us. We experience that it is Jesus who works, who prays, who speaks or is silent, and who is thinking in the 'new person'.

The rainbow illustrates for us the way God's love expresses itself. In clear drops of water, sunlight shines and breaks up into the seven colours of the spectrum. In a person or a community transparent with love through God's word, divine, trinitarian love has varied expressions, both for the individual and in community arrangements.

Love: education in communion

The mark of the first Christian community was that 'they were of one heart and mind, and among them nobody was in need'.[26] They practised the communion of material and spiritual goods; and the same happened when religious institutes started.

Supernatural love has the effect of creating a communion of life. This involves each sharing their own and others' spiritual experiences, joys, trials and successes. Christians cannot but help wanting also to share their material goods with others, all provided by providence or through their work, or what they borrow, because mutual love tends to the highest measure.

Minds and hearts are changed by this. People realize that God is in charge of everything and all is his capital. So the needs of others, other religious orders, other families, the needs of the Church and world become our own as our consciences are touched by this supernatural communion. Everything begins to be shared and to circulate around and nothing remains stuck in one's own room, or in one's own community or religious order; people benefit and the virtue of poverty begins to make sense.

Therefore, in this light, work itself and all its heavy burden is seen as a means to promote and build up communion through service. Love places it within the design of God for the transformation of nature and the whole cosmos, in the divinization of creation. John Paul II in his Apostolic letter to all religious underlined this as the characteristic of those consecrated to God, when he says: 'The transformation of the entire cosmos happens in man's heart and proceeds in harmony with that love which is the substance of consecration.'[27]

Love leads to witnessing

Of the first Christian communities the pagans used to say: 'See how they love one another'. The fire of mutual love attracted others. 'I have come to bring fire to the earth and would that it were alight,'[28] said Jesus.

Fire consumes, gives light and burns up all around it; nor does it need artificially to draw attention to itself; being alight is enough. This is what happens in a community that bases its life on the new commandment of Jesus, where, as *Perfectae Caritatis* says 'It is a true family rejoicing in his presence'.[29] We both feel the joy and relevance of the lives of those living there, and usually we will want such gifts to belong to our own community. The effectiveness of spreading the faith, teaching the Gospel to others, catechesis, assisting groups of visitors to know what we are about, publications of books and magazines is linked more to this living presence of Jesus than to efficient organization or to good methods. 'May they all be one so that the world may believe'.[30] Jesus is living in a community where there is mutual love, so the effectiveness of apostolic methods depends on the witness of brothers or sisters united in his name rather than to the personal qualities of an individual.

Even when we are alone Jesus is the only one who will spread his life and love, and that is the case only insofar as our talking, or writing, or organization, is the expression of communion with our brothers or sisters. We often observe it is more effective for the kingdom of God to have a day of recollection, an apostolic mission or a vocation's exhibition which may be less perfect from an organizational point of view, yet does have this unity and harmony among the organizers, than an imposed and perhaps perfect pastoral strategy without this harmony. In communion with others the fruits of the apostolate can be more easily followed up and, furthermore, we avoid the excesses of an overpersonalized relationship, relying on a particular person. The whole apostolate is guaranteed by the presence of Jesus in the community, by the full communion of the members with each other, and with the person in charge of the community.

Love: formation in spirituality and prayer

St Augustine affirms that charity is the heart of the spiritual life and so by God's grace to remain always in charity results in remaining close to the source of all grace. 'He who remains in love remains in God and God in him.'[31] This is the 'one thing necessary' to which all those consecrated to God are called to witness.

In the Church various ways have been set out leading to this state of soul. Some see it as a ladder to be climbed, or a castle, or the transformation of the caterpillar into the butterfly, or like climbing a mountain peak. Chiara Lubich speaks of a journey on the crest of the mountains, because for a Christian, the departure point is already high up in God. 'We have passed from death to life because we love our brothers', St John wrote,[32] and this being in life, in love, is already being in God. The spiritual life is all about Jesus being formed in us and in others and it results in a continuous effort to love God and our neighbour, to come back to the equilibrium that is Christian love, and to keep it up, right to the end of our lives.

For Christians the journey is a collective one. Jesus asks his disciples to pray always, and he himself because he was always love was always praying, even if sometimes he used to go away and pray alone. If charity is the real driving force of our spiritual life, the different styles of prayer and devotion, whether personal or communal, acquire a completely new dimension. In fact if there is communion and concord as to the intentions to be offered in prayer, Jesus is present, and prayer becomes fascinating and fruitful. Fidelity to prayers such as meditation, divine office, visit to the Blessed Sacrament, rosary, the Eucharist, apart from maintaining our union with God, can continually gain the gift of his constant and effective presence, precisely because it is he himself who is praying in us to the Father.

We know that on the journey to holiness there are trials, difficulties and falls, the continuous struggle between the 'old and new person' in us. We know also that the difficult moments, linked to the suffering, death and forsakenness of

Jesus can be a launching pad to bring us into more intimate communion as children held in the hands of the Father.

Love: education in health

Christian love does more than transform individuals into 'new people', it also renews relationships. St John of the Cross wrote, 'love is the health of the soul',[33] and since Christians are members of one another, this same love insures the health of the Mystical Body. The health of a community is guaranteed by the presence of Jesus. But health needs special sustenance and the extreme lengths to which divine love for humankind goes, is shown by Jesus becoming this food in the Eucharist, the sacrament of unity.

The Eucharist, being Christ's body through the presence of the Holy Spirit has the effect of divinizing the physical body of the Christian, and this is the pledge of its resurrection. All the elements of the universe are concentrated in the human body and so in the human being the Eucharist renders divine both nature and the cosmos.

This outlook means giving great value to the body. After all it is the tangible part of the person and his spirit, and so if we are inspired by supernatural love, we give equal priority to physical as to spiritual life. The human body is the temple of the Holy Spirit and so we should pay attention to all that can assist in the liberation and divinization of the body. We should try to cook with care, use medicines properly, look after the sick and take part in sport and recreation. Whatever the vocation of the 'new person' we cannot forget what St Basil the Great said, 'Man has received the order to become God with the whole of himself.'[34] The place of the body in sickness and in health, in ascetic labour and in rest, must be clarified and not obscured. This kind of care for the body is part of an interest in nature and ecology, since we know the whole of creation is eagerly awaiting the revelation of the children of God.

Supernatural love is particularly concerned where there is

physical or mental illness, and brings sense and purpose to them. When we are confined to a hospital bed, unmoving, it is not all negative. On the contrary, we are then celebrating personally our mass united with Jesus crucified and forsaken. We learn therefore to live out our physical limitations, also psychological and moral ones, and those of others too, in a positive attitude uniting them with Jesus forsaken. Even death is a tunnel leading to the definitive meeting with true and complete life.

Without experience it is perhaps difficult to appreciate the advantage that the spiritual vision of bodily health has for personal holiness and the harmony of a whole community. When we do find the time, because we believe it to be God's will, and make sport, recreation and rest a priority, the body shares with the spirit in the supernatural. Union with God in prayer comes more easily, work is more efficient and the apostolate enjoys greater success.

Love: education in harmony

Incarnated love has an inevitable result: we are involved with and in each other. No longer individuals we are a single people gathered in the name of the Father, Son and Holy Spirit, we are the Church. Love is like blood in the veins of the body. As it circulates all round we feel harmony between all the parts, each with a different function, whether individuals or communities, for the good of the whole. Religious orders especially witness to this in their multiplicity and great variety when love pulsates among them, and each one knows they are Church, the image of the Trinity.

Harmony in the whole Mystical Body affects every individual cell, i.e., families, communities, associations and movements; for love renews everything with which it comes into contact. Even the structures of those communities where the Gospel is lived are renewed. Churches and religious houses, our homes and centres begin to reflect harmony. The furniture, as well as the clothes people wear, express

147

a profound harmony within the sons and daughters of God. At the time of St Francis of Assisi, the ideal of poverty, his ideal, shone out in his centres and houses from the clothes of his followers. Love, incarnated in harmony, can truly bring a revolution if our attention is awoken to the order and maintenance of the house, and in a simple care for our clothing. It gives a particularly eloquent witness that God the Holy Trinity is not only perfect goodness and holiness, but he is harmony and beauty too.

Love: education in wisdom

In Christian experience the truth has a name, Christ. It is not an idea but a person who in the incarnation communicated himself to humankind. Therefore no one can possess the truth alone, or by studying it in books. We can only live the truth together as a body, sharing together in this event. For Christians it is more accurate to say they are possessed by the truth, by the person of Jesus living in them. When Jesus lives in the Christian he gives the possibility of seeing things with God's eyes, wisdom, a gift from God, who interprets facts, events and history.

To reach wisdom, the 'new person' has an obligatory journey to make; to trust wholly in the lived word of God rather than in any personal intelligence or induced self control. In the light of wisdom, studying the various branches of knowledge is a very useful instrument for a more profound research into 'created wisdom', as it is known, which is present in all that is real. So we can have dialogue with people of other cultures to understand the seeds of the Word in them also.

How are we to possess wisdom? If as St Francis of Sales states, 'wisdom is an effect of love',[35] a primary way among those who are studying or engaged in intellectual research is the circulation of charity which generates the presence of Jesus. It is necessary also to live in our personal lives that moment of Jesus abandoned on the cross, when he became pure wisdom, revealing in its fullness the mystery

148

of mysteries, trinitarian love.

Everyone is called to participate in wisdom quite apart from any commitment to study. Yet it is precisely love that leads us to grasp the importance of time spent in study for the harmonious growth of all and of being up-dated in our own specific professional field.

Love: education in participation

In the first Christian communities, the letters of Paul did the rounds, faith was renewed as they shared news, joys, sorrows and difficulties both of individuals and communities. The same applies for us, the same sense of family, when in a Province or entire religious order, news and views are sent around. The fact is that love builds up family, and in this day and age we have the excitement of all modern communication systems to ensure it happens. Happiness at good news is multiplied by a postcard sent out of love. When somebody is confused, love can prompt a letter or a telephone call, assuring our compassion and involvement.

The result? The community grows more united, which is precisely what the 'new person' desires. Unity grows between different religious orders, a Church in relation to other Churches, and the world around us grows more open and friendly. The dream of Jesus, 'that all may be one' can become a reality in our day as the time is ripe and the means of communication are available.

Conclusion

These notes have concentrated on the integrated formation of the person united in body and soul, heart and conscience, intellect and will, and particularly on the development of three elements which mark the DNA of the 'new person'.

Reaching maturity is a dynamic evolution because it is an ideal to be achieved and never an intermediate stage. It is eschatological for the Christian, because we will then attain 'mature manhood to the measure of the stature of the fullness of Christ'.[36]

For an integrated development of the person, we believe the three elements we have covered are essential. The first is the foundation, the sense of being human in re-establishing the relationship with the Father. The second allows people to become who they are meant to be in society, enlarging the personality and relating to others in the image of the Trinity. The third lets the 'new person' develop in an integrated way in the practicalities of daily life, coping with tensions and overcoming them, in the balance of all the aspects of living. An integrated formation of the person means not over-emphasizing a particular aspect at the expense of others, for example the individual dimension of the person to the detriment of the social, or vice-versa.

For the 'new person' to become truly a person, fully herself or himself in Jesus, two sources of light illuminating the way are needed: we could call them the two fires which forge the 'new person'. They are 'an intimate union with God within, listening to the voice of conscience, and with God without, present in the collectivity, Jesus in our midst'. 'Two fires: Jesus within us, Jesus among us'. The first Christian personality to be formed at this kind of school was Mary, 'Mary, at her Nazareth home lived between two fires, the Holy Spirit who was the spiritual director of her soul, and Jesus, God, who was her son'.[37]

Formation in Christian life is achieved in this way, therefore, as an individual and as a member of a community. When communal holiness improves so does individual sanctity, and when there is a growth in individual sanctity there is improvement among everybody.

At the start of the spiritual experience of Chiara Lubich and her companions (in an experience of dynamic unity and distinction, with the harmony of the practical aspects of life), she wrote to her companions: 'You will become completely different from each other and yet totally identical, because you will be Jesus ... It will be a bit like a repeat of the Holy Trinity ... many completely distinct personalities like the saints, yet one because in each Christ will be living.'[38]

REFERENCES
1. 'Prossemics' is the term coined by Edward T. Hall in his book *The Hidden Dimension (La dimensione nascosta: Ed. Bompiano, Milano 1973)*. It deals with gathering observations and theories about the use of space for man, understood as specifically linked with culture.

Franz Boas more than fifty years previously had already set up the anthropological basis for this science. Edward Sapir and Leonard Blomfield perfected it and it was confirmed by Lee Whorf.

'Prossemics' is the science that leads to an understanding of the significance of personal and social space within a culture, offering means to evaluate the reciprocal conditioning among human beings and the use of vital space in various cultures.
2. *Redemptor Hominis*, John Paul II 10.
3. *Gaudium et Spes*, 22.
4. *God among Men*, Pasquale Foresi, New City, London 1974 pp 72–85.
5. *Appunti di Filosofia*, P. Foresi, Città Nuova, Rome, pp. 60–61, 133–145, 156–157.
6. *Song of the Birds*, Anthony di Mello.
7. *Psychological Types*, C J Jung. (Italian edt. *Tipi psicologici*, Newton Compton Italiana, 1970 p. 53).
8. cf. Rom. 8:29.
9. *Redemptor Hominis op. cit.* 8.
10. *Familiaris Consortio*, Apostolic exhortation of John Paul II, 11. 11. Idem.
12. *Trinità e mistero dell'esistenza*. J Danielou, Queriniana, Brescia 1969. pp. 13; 49; 54.
13. *De variis difficilibus locis*, P. G. 91, 1309.
14. *Gesù in mezzo nel pensiero di Chiara Lubich*, J. Povilus. Città Nuova, Rome 1981, pp. 67–68 (S. C. R. 2/12/'46)
15. *La Trinità come storia*, Bruno Forte Edizione Paoline 1985 p.177.
16. *Psicoanalisi e personalita'* by J. Nuttin. Edizione Paoline, Roma-Alba 1960 pp. 303–305.

17. *Revolution personnaliste et communautaire*, I. E. Mounier p. 383.
18. J Povilus, op. cit.
19. *La personne du Christ, recherche ontologique*, J. Galot. Italian transl. *La persona di Cristo*, Assisi 1979.
20. *Comm. in Matth.*, Origen, XIV, 7 ff. PG. 1187.
21. *Familiaris Consortio*, John Paul II. 37.
22. cf. Matt. 10:39.
23. J. Nuttin, *op. cit.* p. 309.
24. Notebooks from the volume, *Literaturae nasledstvo*, F. Dostoevsky. Moscow 1971.
25. Some humanist philosophers, psychologists and psychiatrists have shown interest in this aspect of the maturing of the person. See J. Nuttin *op. cit.* 'We have shown that the personality fully expands when it goes out of itself to give itself to others. The renunciation of the ego in this sense is the vital experience of the self.' (*Journal Metaphysique* by G. Marcel, Gallimard, Paris 1927 p. 309, cf. also p. 228.) 'It is indeed paradoxical: each one of us wants to be ourselves and we see in ourselves and in the others with whom there is a relationship a progressive modification. This means that if I want to encourage the personal growth of others in relationship with me, I myself must grow, and although this is painful it leads to my enrichment.'

'In contradiction to a superficial logic one receives by giving; or better, giving is already a way of receiving.' (*Homo Viator* by G. Marcel, Borla, Torino 1967 p. 170). cf. J. Povilus op. cit. S.C.R. 27/3/1950, *Lido di Ostia* which goes like this: 'The three live uniting themselves by their nature, by loving and uniting themselves (noughting themselves), they find themselves. The three make themselves one out of love, and in that unique love they find themselves again.

Analogically for us: noughting ourselves totally out of love, so that we become one, we flower again, equal though distinct.

Our human personality, far from being reduced to nothing by the divine, is made stronger.'
26. Acts. 4:34
27. *Redemptionis donum*, John Paul II, 9.
28. cf. Luke 12:49.
29. *Perfectae Caritatis*, 15.
30. cf. John 17:21.
31. cf. 1 John 4:16.
32. 1 John 3:14.
33. Saint John of the Cross, *Spiritual Canticle*, 11.
34. Gregory Nazianzen, *In laudem Basilii*, PG. 36: 560.

35. *Introduction to the devout life*, Francis de Sales. (Italian edition *La Vita di perfezione*, Edizione Paoline, IV, p. 211)
36. cf. Eph. 4:13.
37. J. Povilus op. cit. Chiara Lubich is quoted on p 144, note 64.
38. Idem. p. 72, note 16.

EXPERIENCES

The Experience of the Formation Community of the Oblates of Mary Immaculate (Vermicino, Italy)

A 'formation community' of the Oblates of Mary Immaculate has 39 young religious who are preparing for final profession. Their experience is based on 'co-responsibility' in the light of their rule which explains that 'all (the teachers and those in formation) are disciples of the same Lord.'

Some of these young men explain how co-responsibility is lived out in the various practical aspects of life in community: the financial side and the use of money, physical health and rest, taking care of each person and of the environment, formation and spiritual life, pastoral work, doctrinal studies.

Their experience witnesses that making this effort so that 'all may be achieved in mutual love and in unity' means that these practical aspects work together for the integrated human and supernatural formation of each person and of the community.

The community of Oblates of Vermicino (near Rome) is a 'formation community'. At the moment [January 1988] it consists of five priests, three brothers and 39 young religious in vows who are preparing for final profession and priesthood.

Our community life, made up of many facets and very varied, is marked by 'co-responsibility' as suggested by our rule, which explains 'the teachers and those in formation are all disciples of the same Lord and they make a single community.' (Chapter 51) Taking charge of so many aspects that make up and give life to the community is, therefore, entrusted largely to the young people themselves, who find they do not merely perform a service for others, but also give a practical contribution by sharing fully in the experience of formation in the entire community.

We can discern different areas of formation in this experience, which is like a journey. The first concerns human formation, expressed in work, in the development of the gifts and personal aptitudes of the students, in their maturing affectivity, in their conduct in the house and in the care of their health.

For example, to experience the truth of the words of the Gospel: 'Seek first the kingdom of God and all the rest will be given to you' and so to see the daily intervention of providence, is a powerful experience. It affects, in the first instance, the young students to whom the accounts are entrusted, but then, also, all the others.

Managing the accounts of a religious community of about 50 is not the whole story. There is also the maintenance of the building, the cleaning of the outside area shared by everybody, and co-operation with the nuns who are working in the kitchen and the laundry. Such activity is a continual source of building up valuable personal relationships. It is even more constructive when little difficulties arise. All helps in our constant effort towards mutual love.

We want this love to mark all our day. A practical expression of it is when we are doing the shopping, and we find out what each person's needs are, or if we should buy something for the house. Together we look at what each person suggests and what a particular need might be and then decide, bearing in mind also our call to poverty. Each person is responsible individually and we all are responsible together.

In this way, the person who is bursar is helped to fulfil his task. He is not the person to whom every burden and every decision is delegated. Everyone is involved in making plans, in seeing things get done and in acquiring what is needed. Of course, he is the one who gathers together all the suggestions, the individual needs, and he masterminds various arrangements. There is common involvement, which spills over outside the community. We all try to support the poor people who come to the door and the gypsies who ask our help.

We have this 'financial aspect based on life', and from that we gain an understanding of the role of physical health and sport in such a religious community. Often a religious community, with its set framework and established structures, rather prevents or puts conditions on any efforts in that direction. Yet no community should really limit its sights in this area simply to avoid illness.

The care and love for our brother encourages us to look for and to want his good, so we try to find opportunities to engage in sport. An afternoon a week is set aside and each person is asked not to be absent, despite tiredness, or work, or studying, since that may perhaps prevent the others enjoying their team game or their football match.

Also we have time to relax on days off; we might go on an excursion or into the countryside together. They are also important moments to share experiences, to talk with each other, and to explain plans or outline difficulties.

We plan our summer holidays in this way too; we go in small groups. Each suggests what kind of thing they would like, and this makes it feel like a family, and encourages the different gifts of each person.

In community, illness also is a unique chance to share with and to live with the other person. In fact one brother in the community is semi-paralysed and needs assistance. This is a constant exercise which helps love grow. Other religious needing rest or who are ill, are welcomed into the community, and every time it makes us appreciate the person quite other than his abilities, and to love him as he is.

A special contribution to our formation is given by the Franciscan Sisters of the Poor who have been called to offer their services with our community, especially in the kitchen, which is a place of constant coming and going. Some go there for a snack, others to lay the tables or wash up. Also relatives, friends and guests seem to gravitate there, so among all the pots and pans there is the chance to make practical the spirit of charity of their foundress Mother Francesca Schervier, in welcoming all those whom they meet. Their foundress, working together with ours, Blessed Eugene de Mazenod through their followers in religious life can, we hope, realize their unity 'on earth as it is in heaven.' Sister Regina used to say: 'being in the kitchen is a continuous effort, which culminates in the evening during mass. I place in the chalice all the joys and sufferings of those I have met, my own mistakes and all the tirednesses, and the thanksgiving to God for the miracles that Jesus in the midst is doing. I myself feel that certainty that I am making my genuine contribution in my daily work and prayer in this place, for the formation of these future missionaries and priests, so that the testament of Jesus "that all may be one" may be fulfilled.'

Daily and repetitive activities have to be done. Finding the meaning that goes beyond these household tasks comes from believing that everything is a gift, is the love of God: our own person, the brothers, the house, the time we have at our disposal. As we take care of every single aspect we mature in realizing that all has been given and entrusted to each single person for the good of the whole community; their gifts, their abilities, their plans and so on.

Furnishing a place in a simple and at the same time beautiful way, and being involved in looking after and cleaning the various parts of the house in which we live, allows the other person to feel more at ease and welcomed in a home that each one feels their own, and we can truly say is ours.

Sometimes the walls themselves manifest the communion among those who live there. Even if the harmony that we find there has in a certain sense to be constructed, in a structural sense as well as metaphorically. For this reason four groups have been formed in the community and to each, a particular sector of the house has been entrusted. One looks after the secretarial work, another is concerned with guests, making them feel welcome; then there is the liturgy and all that involves, the organizing of the 'shows' which we lay on for feast days, for missions and so forth.

In this work, as in all others, what cements it together is the effort to do it with love, for it is from our unity that the harmony comes. Unity is the product of our being side by side, living for each other.

Our brother missionaries in far off places are not able to participate literally in community life but we want to maintain a bond of unity with them, and with others who do not live with us. For this, as for our efforts to explain this supernatural and deep sharing with those outside the house, the mass media is an essential.

In the community some are involved more directly with tape-recorders, slide shows, film editing. But we try to involve everyone in the modern means of communication and with what they can offer. It is helpful to learn about film projectors, cameras, video-recorders, in working groups.

A second area of formation which we concentrate on is spiritual. This too is a community effort; in fact, if we find that the human development of the individual is encouraged in work and through the community responsibilities, then spiritual formation is all the more clearly to be understood in the context of the community.

In the groups into which the community is divided, there are moments for sharing experiences of what we have done, for listening, for giving to others our reflections on the meditations, for understanding the homilies more fully, for the verification in daily life of what we listen to: in other words, for growth together.

The culminating moment of the day is the evening mass when we can all be present to reflect and meditate together.

Development within the community enriches the individual. This too is a real spiritual journey, and so it also has various stages. Each person develops on a different time-scale, but we find out that after the fervour of the novitiate, all those things that at first attracted us to the religious life can become monotonous and repetitive.

The time has come perhaps when we are called to make a truer and more decisive choice of God. Religious life can then regain the radical purity and completeness of its ideal.

The effect of this: in proportion to our relationship with God, relationships with the brothers, and also with our Superior, are deepened. Through the Superior we are called to come face to face with the clear expression of the will of God.

Even though this journey has to be undertaken by the individual alone, the spiritual and practical support, the help and involvement of the brothers, in a relationship of communion with all the checks and balances of relationships, make this journey the outcome of a spiritual formation that is communitarian.

A third area is the apostolate, in accord with the missionary vocation of this religious family and in tune with our founder's wishes, i.e. Blessed Eugene de Mazenod: he wanted

158

numbered only 3, but the next year there were already 12 and in 1977, 20 or so.

As the initiative gradually developed, on the one hand the religious came to realize that Montericco was too far from the centre of the Work of Mary which is near Rome. On the other hand, those at the Centre appreciated the initiative and decided to take more direct responsibility for it. Accordingly it was thought advisable to look for a house in the district of Castelli, near Rome. The Capuchin house at Albano was found. In this way what had been the 'School of Religious of the Movement for Religious' became the 'School of the Work of Mary for Religious'. Chiara Lubich gave it the name *Charis School* and a Word of Life: *Aemulamini charismata meliora* (Earnestly desire the higher gifts) (1 Cor. 12:31).

In the autumn of 1981, an opportunity arose of leasing the Villa Andrea at Castelgandolfo – the summer villa of the College of St Josaphat of the Ukrainians. The Charis School was transferred to it, so from Albano it moved to Castelgandolfo. Then in October of 1986 it moved to Loppiano, near Florence. Here Chiara gave it the new name of *Claritas School*. At Loppiano it is with the schools of the other branches of the Movement and is part of Loppiano's one large school, an integral part of the life of the permanent Mariapolis there.[1]

During the twelve years of its life, more than a thousand religious have passed through it, from about 130 different institutes. Of these only about 100 stayed more than five months, and almost half stayed less than one month. The number of those present at any one time varied from 15 to 25 or 30 at Albano, from 10 to 20 at Castelgandolfo, from 5 to 15 at Loppiano.

2. Almost every week there are arrivals and departures; some come for a more thorough acquaintance with a life they have known and loved for a long time already; some come for a first experience of it; and there are even some who drop in more or less by chance. In such a situation it is obviously impossible to follow fixed and progressive half-yearly courses. We have to adapt ourselves week by week to the composition of the group, with a long term

and a short term programme in concentric cycles around the points of spirituality, history and organisation of the Movement. These are arranged so that those who stay only a short while may gain a complete, if summary, knowledge of some one subject, while those who stay longer will not be obliged to repeat anything.

That is possible, because our school is not so much a 'school of culture' but a 'school of life'. Indeed, the continual need to adapt ourselves to our actual situation lays greater emphasis on the aspect of 'life' than on that of 'culture'. This, in the last resort, is providential, since it is 'life' rather than 'culture' that religious need, partly because of the unconscious tendency to transform life into theory rather than theory into life.

3. The background against which we try to organize our programme and our life in its various expressions and activities, is constituted by Matt. 18:20: 'Where two or three gather together in my name, I am there among them'. Against this background we strive, and help one another, to live and grow in Christ, living week by week one of his sayings (the Word of Life as we call it) and sharing every day our experiences with one another.

4. From what the participants say and write, I can state, I think, that their experience of the school is truly positive and that it brings about in religious a real spiritual maturing, not so much in the sense of a better intellectual understanding of the Gospel, of the charism of their founder and of their institute, as rather in the sense of a deeper and living involvement in the spirit of the Gospel, of their founder and of their institute. To put it briefly, I can, I think, say that by strengthening their personal and communitarian self-awareness the very root of every charism, and therefore of every vocation, is strengthened.

That emerges clearly, I think, from letters we have received from religious who have passed through the school. These are but a few extracts:

– While before for me the Gospel was too often something which I presupposed and which I only took seriously in part, now after the experience of the school it has become my life, the whole approach for living out my brotherhood with others.

– These months in the school for religious have been among the most beautiful of my life. Living with Jesus the teacher present among us united in his name, I feel we have shared the experience of the first disciples. Often he has inflamed my heart, explained the Gospel to me and taught me to live his word each day. Again it is he who in this school has taught me to recognize and love him in suffering, in the ordinary sufferings of daily work, in the suffering of having to learn Italian, in the suffering of having to put aside my own ideas to forge them into unity. Finally he led me to become more and more aware of his life within me fed by the eucharist which allows me to be another Jesus. I feel this is the heart and the substance of all my life, also my religious life.

– It is difficult to explain what the school meant for me; it has been a very great grace for my life and for that of my institute. During these months I have become aware that the spirituality of unity is not something added on to my vocation as a brother of St Gabriel but together with it forms a single whole. Each day I try to choose God first of all, that is to allow Jesus to grow in me by living the Word of Life. Only this choice gives sense to my religious life, to my apostolate, to my prayer, to my community life, to my poverty, to my obedience and to my chastity.

– This is the fruit of the school; an indissoluble bond with Jesus crucified and forsaken. Now he is no longer the one I look for and welcome with joy when he comes under the aspect of suffering, but he is love incarnate who has entered my life and always wants to live with me.

– The first fruit of the school has been that of recognizing that I had not yet made a radical choice of God. For example I was still very attached to my work. Now it seems to me that I am ready to change my work every time it is God's will to do so.

— I am going back to Spain after having passed seven months in the school at Albano. I can sincerely say that this experience has been the most powerful thing that has ever happened to me. At the beginning there were only few of us, but I have had the clear sensation that this type of experience of common life among members of different orders and congregations is something quite unique in the history of the Church. We were united by one single reality, God. It seems to me that in us, the expressions of different charisms of religious life, I can see and understand again the whole of the Gospel brought back to unity. Through Jesus I have understood my own founder as if for the very first time.

— We are in a school where it is a question of living the Gospel radically and, faced by that, everything seems new and encourages you to begin again. In this school, life comes before speaking, and there is only one reference point: Jesus Christ.

5. I have been asked what these years at the Charis School and the Claritas School have meant for me. How have I grown in Jesus as a Christian and as a religious?

It is rather hard to say. Whereas for others I can, I think, state with relative tranquillity that their stay at the school meant a progress, in regard to myself I do not know what to say. In some ways I seem to have made progress, for example I am less anxious in the face of unforeseen events, with a more tranquil acceptance of my limitations and my fragility, less vulnerability in regard to what is said or thought of me, greater straightforwardness in my relations with others, a greater readiness to see the positive side of events and persons, and a greater ability to understand and accept others.

But is all this the effect of real growth in Christ, or is it only an effect of age, diminished promptitude and vitality in reflexes, and a better state of health? I have the impression that often my virtue is nothing but good health.

Indeed, I must say that when sometimes, rarely, I stop to draw up a balance sheet of my life and remember the eagerness of my early days, I have the impression that I have gone backwards rather than forwards. But let us leave it to God to judge. Perhaps we can apply what St Paul says about 'seeing in a mirror dimly' (1 Cor. 13:12) to this case too. Now, of course, the mirror reflects things upside down, so that what appears below is really above and what appears regression is really progression. However that may be, 'All I can say is this: forgetting what is behind me, and reaching out for that which lies ahead, I press on, hoping to take hold of him who has taken hold of me . . . ' (cf. Phil. 3: 12, 13).

What happened at Fongumetaw (Cameroon)

Another characteristic story set in the context of a small nucleus of religious of different institutes who have been allowed by their Superiors to be at the disposal of the Work of Mary so that they may be an instrument to build communion for religious who follow the spirituality of unity (more than 1,000) spread in the various African countries.

It is a service carried out in a very simple way (through letters, through a few days or even one day of rest spent together) but which is seen to be extremely precious, above all in Africa, where so often loneliness is a big problem, and work usually is far too heavy.

My name is Mario and I belong to the missionary congregation of the Oblates of Mary Immaculate. I have been in the Western Cameroon for five years at Fongumetaw, together with Fr Celso who is also an Oblate and with Fr Bernold a Franciscan of the Friars Minor from Germany.

We make up a small community at the service of religious who participate in the spirituality of the Work of Mary and who are spread in almost all the countries of Africa below the Sahara.

A few years ago, in fact in 1976, the Work of Mary in Africa asked if it would be possible to have some religious who could keep permanently in contact with the missionaries who already knew the Movement and who wanted to deepen their understanding of its spirituality.

Our Superiors invited us therefore to go to the Cameroon

165

to undertake this task in service of the Church in Africa. There are about 1,000 religious who know the Movement there, and with 300 we have a personal relationship, even if sometimes we maintain it only by letter. On the mission, above all in the most isolated places, the arrival of a letter has a much greater importance than it could have in Europe. Through this method we reach many of our brothers and with them we try to grow together, and to go ahead confirming with each other our vocation to which God has called us and is calling us. Often they feel alone in a huge territory far from any town and their letters are burdened by their many worries and sufferings as well as with the large or small joys they experience. In front of the fire in the evening (we are living at a height of 1,500 metres), reading together the letters that have come, we share in their joys and their pains. When we reply to the letters we try not so much to give solutions to their problems, as to share our own small experiences lived day by day in community. We too have to overcome our difficulties as they do by means of mutual communion, always embracing Jesus crucified.

Apart from this, every two months we write a circular letter in which we copy some paragraphs of the letters we have received from religious (it is usually about 30 each month) which we then send to all those with whom we are in touch, so that life can circulate and be shared for the building up for everybody. Different religious have written to us quoting from one or other paragraph which has helped them to live, or to overcome a particular difficult moment of their life.

Some of them have been to visit us to share our life. It is a great help that we live in a pleasant climate (we are in fact on a mountain, but on the equator) and these religious have been able to spend a longer or shorter period of time with us. This strengthens them in body and in spirit, and so they can take up again their missionary activity with a new enthusiasm. All of us have Jesus as our aim and we experience his presence among two or more, even from different congregations and orders.

This is what a Capuchin missionary priest wrote for us while he was with us in Fongumetaw, and before going back to central Africa.

166

I am very happy to live here with you for a few days so that I can immerse myself in communion and unity. It is absolutely necessary for me to enter into this life of communion or else I feel as though I will die. Yes: in communion, which means sharing and giving oneself, life comes from that; Jesus himself is present and you feel renewed, refreshed in spirit. The last two years my work has been far too heavy but now I am convinced that I simply must reserve more time for this life of communion so that my work as a missionary and evangelizer may be more authentic.

These few days with you at Fongumetaw have had a strange effect on me. My heart clearly tells me that the definitive choice of God is for me a necessity, and I must choose him again without delay. Yet again in this atmosphere of unity I realise fully that God still loves me despite all my failures. It was just the right time to choose God as everything in my life.

Here in Africa time flies by and one grows old prematurely, I have felt the urgent need to join you on this journey towards holiness by living the Word in the present moment more intensely. What is more, all the numerous difficulties that I have experienced these past two years I now see are instruments in the hands of the Father who is calling me to conversion of heart, and to a more intimate communion with him.

REFERENCES
1. A permanent Mariapolis, like the Focolare Movement's summer gatherings which are also called 'Mariapolis', seeks to be a piece of society in which the Gospel is lived day in day out. (Mariapolis means 'City of Mary'.)

V THE DYNAMICS OF GROWTH IN THE SPIRIT

To grow to the measure of the stature of Christ

Fr Bonaventure Marinelli OFM Cap.

The feast of the Epiphany[1] reminds us that the Magi came from the East to adore Jesus. On that occasion God's plan for humanity was disclosed, his plan to call the pagans to share the same inheritance as the chosen people, to form with them the same Body. This plan had been concealed from previous generations, and has now been revealed to the holy apostles and prophets (as St Paul says in the 2nd reading of the feast). The feast of the Epiphany recalls a past event, but it celebrates a dimension of salvation history which is always present, a dimension in which we are involved. We too have been called to share the same inheritance, to form the one body of Christ.

The Epiphany therefore celebrates the process of salvation: God's initiative and human response. Into the dough of humanity God has thrown the leaven of his Son. Like leavened dough, humanity begins to rise, allowing itself to be penetrated by this new life. It sets out to express this new life fully.

2. The liturgy of the Epiphany throws light upon the social aspect of this process. The peoples converge on Jerusalem with their gifts (1st reading); the pagans are called to form the one Body of Christ (2nd reading); all nations and races find their unity by gathering together towards Jesus. However, this presupposes the individual dimension; each people draws close to Jesus to the extent that the individual members draw close to Jesus.

It is obvious that this journey towards Jesus is spiritual, not geographical. We draw close to Jesus to the extent that we allow ourselves to be penetrated and illuminated by his light, by his word, by him. We draw close to him to the extent that we are clothed with Christ, that we grow in him and he grows in us.

Every human group has to travel a great distance if it is to arrive at Jesus and be enlightened by him, if it is to become his presence, progressively revealing him. This distance is what separates two different ways of living together. On one hand, there is a living together which is full of tension, of divisions, of conflict which can be camouflaged or even structured, a life in common held together, for the most part, by structures and common interests. On the other hand, there is a life in common which is a living unity 'in the name of Jesus'. This is permeated by love. It is a life in which Jesus can express himself and reveal himself. A group will cross the distance between these two life-styles if, and only to the extent that, its members undertake to do so. They must first cross the terrain of the old self, with all that this implies, before they enter into the promised land of the new self, who is Jesus.

The Epiphany celebrates the dynamic process of the Kingdom of God in us (clothed with Christ), and in our midst (many in one Body). It is the feast of gathering together in Christ all peoples, all the human race, all the members of every community; it is the feast of the convergence in Christ of every aspect of life, of all human powers of life – until humanity reaches the fullness of its stature, until the final Epiphany, when Christ will be all in all, and all shall be one in him.

3. Scripture presents the Christian life as a passage from the reign of law to the reign of grace. Since we are children, we are still being taught until we come of age (Gal. 3:24 f). 'The night is far gone, the day is at hand' (Rom. 13:12). With our baptism, the night has passed, but it is not yet day time. Through baptism we are the children of God in Jesus, but we are still minors. Baptism has given us a new life, but only in seed; this new life must be developed.

St Paul insists very strongly on our personal and communal life in Christ. And he requires that we live this life also in our way of behaving and acting; in fact, we must be increasingly like this. From the way in which he expresses himself, it seems clear that for him baptism is not a magic rite that transforms the

169

individual and the community in a complete, final way, as if it cast a spell. On the contrary, baptism is only the beginning of a gradual process of transformation and growth. It is the fruit of the powerful interaction of the Holy Spirit, who is the vital force of this new life, and our personal and communal efforts.

On the part of the individual, this does not mean doing things, launching oneself into activity, observing laws and commandments, behaving according to Christian customs and practices. It means being Christians, and being always more Christian, that is, being other Christs, love incarnate.

On the part of the community, it does not mean so much being well organized according to Canon Law and the constitutions of each institute. It means being the Body of Christ, being always more and more the Body of Christ, mutual love incarnate – a lived unity which makes real what Jesus promised: 'Where two or three are gathered in my name, there am I in the midst of them' (Matt. 18:20).

Eucharistic consecration takes place in a moment: it is enough that the bread be bread. Our transformation into Christ, however, is progressive. It lasts for a lifetime, and will probably require an extra while in Purgatory.

4. It is important that we realize that, whatever our age, we have not arrived at our destination. We are still becoming what we ought to be. We are always in formation, even if we are a hundred years old, even if we are in charge of formation in our institute. We have to be, rather than do: to be Jesus 'love incarnate', in such a way that what we do gives expression to him rather than to ourselves. That is why we must constantly compare ourselves with him, with his word, with his example. We must ask ourselves what would be his thoughts, his feelings, his behaviour in each situation, and we must try to shape up to what the Spirit says within us.

We have to adopt the spiritual attitude of St Paul. 'Imitate me, then, just as I imitate Christ' (1 Cor. 11:1), he encourages us; and he offers himself as an example: 'I do not claim that I have already succeeded . . . the one thing I do, however, is to forget what is behind me and do my best to reach what is ahead. So I run straight towards the goal in order to win the prize, which is God's call through Christ Jesus to the life above'

(Phil. 3: 12–14). Saul, who was seized by Christ on the road to Damascus, becomes Paul who presses forward to try to lay hold of Christ, who slips away before him like an unattainable ideal. At the very least, Paul tries to lessen the gap between his way of living, of acting and reacting, and that of Jesus. This Paul is the model for what must be our spiritual outlook. If we maintain this attitude, we will progress day by day, we will grow in Jesus. We will succeed in seeing the love of God not only in the beauty of created things, in the successful result of some activity, in rich insights and inspiration, in the affection and kindness of our brothers and sisters. We will also see the love of God in disasters, in suffering, in failure, aridity, misunderstanding.

Our sensitivity to the will of God will increase. We will recognize it not only in explicit commands, in laws, in the great events of history. We will see it in moments of inspiration, in the ordinary events of each day. We will not only accept the will of God; we will seek it out and love it. We will not only carry it out, but live it in such a way that we identify with it ever more closely.

Gradually, as God's will becomes everything for us, we will develop an awareness that is ever more acute and forceful that the essence of God's will for us is that we ourselves are love in the concrete circumstances of our lives. And this love will grow stronger and spread. It will become more natural and spontaneous for us to love everyone, to love first, to love without expecting results or anything in return, to love in a concrete way, seizing opportunities to console, to help, to serve, to waste time with someone, to set aside our plans, our life. We will be able to keep eyes and ears open to our brothers and sisters, even when we feel crushed by the effort, torn apart in body and soul, sunk in the darkness of agony and the feeling of failure and desolation.

In a parallel manner, our relationship with the Word of God will develop. From being an object of study and meditation, it will become a call to concrete action. Instead of being a slogan, something proposed to us, it will become a living communion with the essential Word, Jesus. We will allow ourselves to be penetrated by him, to let him live in us. In a similar way our relationship with the eucharist will mature: from faith in the presence of Jesus and the cult of adoration, it will develop a practical insight into the meaning of the Sacrament, through which Jesus says to us: 'I am your life: live me!'

5. Whatever our community may be like, even if it is the most beautiful in the world, it has not yet arrived at perfection: it, too, is always on the road towards what it should be. It is always in formation. Every member, even the most recent novice, has a responsibility to make his own contribution to its formation as the Body of Christ.

Grateful for the brothers that the Lord has given us, and for the community in which he has placed us, we must strive to make it even more beautiful, ever more the living, harmonious Body of Christ, a community increasingly 'united in his name'. We must not allow ourselves to lose our bearings and wander off course because of all that needs to be done, all the way that has to be travelled. We must strive, by our presence and behaviour, to ease and make supernatural our relationships with one another, gradually smoothing out and banishing all that divides, strengthening what unites. We have to encourage participation and the spirit of joint responsibility and collaboration. We must increasingly involve the others in the effort to lay hold of Jesus personally, and to affirm him in the community, so that it is always he who acts in the activities of the individuals, he who expresses himself in the various features of community life.

6. St Grignon de Montfort says that Jesus will become flesh in us to the extent that he finds Mary in us. The essential Marian devotion is this: to reproduce Mary in ourselves; to make her feelings ours; to adopt her spiritual disposition; to be silent like her, so that the Word may take shape in us and through us; to be empty like her, so that we can be filled by Jesus.

'Trahe nos, post te curremus in odorem unguentorum tuorum'

'Draw us to you, and we will run after you, attracted by the fragrance of your ointment.'

REFERENCES
1. This meditation was given on 6th January the Feast of the Epiphany.

Spiritual Growth in the Formation Journey

Fr. Sante Bisignano OMI

Introduction

1. I want to begin with the Word of God. I turn to Matthew to narrate for us once again the call of some disciples by Jesus. In that call we understand our own, and the significance of being with him, and of being sent to announce the good news.

> As he was walking by the lake of Galilee he saw two brothers, Simon who was called Peter, and his brother Andrew; they were making a cast into the lake with their net for they were fishermen. And he said to them, "Come after me and I will make you fishers of people." And at once they left their nets and followed him.
>
> Going on from there he saw another pair of brothers, James son of Zebedee and his brother John; ... and he called them. And at once, leaving the boat and their father, they followed him.
>
> As Jesus was walking on from there he saw a man named Matthew sitting at the tax office, and he said to him, 'Follow me.' And he got up and followed him. (Matt. 4:18–22; 9:9).

The initiative in meeting with Christ the Lord comes from the love of the Father and of the Son (cf. John 15:9–17, 6) and it changes everything. Peter, James, John, the twelve, began a journey in him and with him. They knew they had been called by name and they were involved together in the fulfilment of the Father's plan of salvation. 'For this is how

173

God loved the world: he gave his only Son, so that everyone who believes in him may not perish but may have eternal life.' 'For God sent his Son into the world not to judge the world, but so that through him the world might be saved.' (John 3:16–17)

The Son, become obedient unto death and to death on the cross, becomes Lord. He has given us the Holy Spirit that we may become 'new creatures', and for society to flower into the family of God.

2. From then Christ has had innumerable followers, spurred on by the Spirit, each with the same passionate longing and aspiration to follow him more closely and to proclaim him to all nations. They have wanted to stay with him, treading the paths of humankind, serving their brothers and sisters with the charity of Christ. They have wanted to know the Father and be united in Christ Jesus to reveal the multiform wisdom of God and the overflowing riches of his love. Augustine, Benedict, Dominic, Francis, Ignatius, Teresa of Avila, Paul of the Cross . . . all our founders belong to this band of followers. We in religious life who are living in this springtime of the Church, are part of it too.

We are looking at today's world with some of the vision of God the Father. The world cries out to us in its suffering, and with its longing for truth and justice. 'Christians are the permanent springtime of humanity', Clement of Alexandria loved to say.

3. To speak of the dynamic of growth in the Spirit is to contemplate this movement of holiness, of communion, and of apostolic charity. We are a part of it in the living history of the Body of Christ. In our loving response to the Spirit, we must try to be involved in the life of the Church as it actually is; for the Spirit continues to pour out his gifts on it abundantly.

It never means withdrawing from our brothers and sisters and from life around us. It does mean serving everyone as would Christ who is 'our life' (cf. Col. 3:4) so that each and everybody may have life and have it to the full.

174

Life in the Spirit is lived in time and space as a member of the Body of Christ: and Mary is Christ's mother. It is a special journey for each person because each is called by name and is loved personally. It is also a journey which we achieve together collectively, it is communitarian, for we are his Body. This Body is 'one' (cf. 1 Cor. 12:12), in continuous growth to full maturity: striving to be perfect in unity as the Father and the Son. (cf. John 17: 11, 21, 23)

Formation of the new generation, as permanent formation, requires that we revive this vision of things as they are. Precisely because 'the Word became flesh' (John 1:14) all this is possible. It is possible to achieve the deepest union with God while travelling through our world's history, and it is possible to achieve an increasing communion among ourselves in virtue of his presence (cf. Matt. 18:20). So we can be a prophetic sign, the Word which gives light, the charity where God is at home.

4. Against this background I would like to draw attention to some of the fundamental points in the dynamic of spiritual growth. They are both goals to be achieved and an explanation of the principles of formation. I will group them in two parts. In the first we will examine in a narrative way the foundations of growth in the Spirit. In the second I will try to trace its itinerary in the light of the experience of Mary, mother of the Church and of humankind.

I The foundations of growth in the Spirit

1. An objective vision of life according to the Spirit, and its dynamic, is the starting point for adequate formation. We need it to follow the right path in the right direction. It is a journey of growth in consecration to the Lord, in union with him, conforming to him, and in full communion with our brothers and sisters. (cf. Eph. 4: 15–16) It is a process of continuous maturing, as we progressively understand more about sharing in the gift that he (Jesus) makes of himself to

the Father, and his brotherly service of humankind. At the same time we must always remain in conformity with the charism of our foundation. For religious, being 'clothed in Christ' (cf. Rom. 13:14 – Gal. 3:27 – Eph. 4:24) in his poverty, his love, his obedience is the essential aim of life.

Religious in fact, because of their vocation, live for 'God above', and collaborate in the work of redemption and the construction of the kingdom (cf. PC 5) according to the style of the charism of the founder. Following Christ is the dynamic reality that unifies a person and establishes their identity.

This life according to the Spirit is the life of the person become a 'new creation' in baptism, who also participates in 'religious consecration' in the charism of the founder. It is a life whose features blossom by sharing in the mystery of the death and resurrection of Christ, lived in the ecclesial community. Life in the Spirit is as it were a movement between the 'already' and the 'not yet' and it is enriched by the gifts which the Holy Spirit liberally gives continually to the people of God along its journey. The dynamic of life in the Spirit is one of growth of the interior being which 'is renewed day by day'. (2 Cor. 4:16) 'Since we are living by the Spirit, let our behaviour be guided by the Spirit.' (Gal. 5:25)

To describe this life is to narrate our personal story, and to narrate it as Church. In a certain sense it is to remind ourselves of our meeting with Christ: to explain why he appealed to us, what he proposed, and what he asked for; then to describe our response in belonging to him. This experience is both personal and communal, it corresponds to our individual personality, and to our social experience. It will help us to understand something of the journey for the new generations by a kind of similarity between us. Also it will help us to understand the long journey undertaken by the person who has known the stages of the spiritual life for some time, and has felt an increasing and growing passion for the Church and the kingdom,

'Reminding ourselves' means to celebrate the interior meeting with Christ's love, from which the call to the evangelical counsels arises. 'Jesus looked steadily at him and he was filled with love for him'. (Mark 10:21) It means welcoming his redemptive love which forms us as his sons and daughters and members of his Body, and which opens our vision on humankind and teaches us to love with the love with which he loves every creature.

Helping the younger generations, or helping us adults, involves leading us together to gaze on Christ the Lord and to let that vision penetrate deeply within each person. It means letting him call us anew 'by name', through his love. Without this experience of divine love no journey in the Spirit can begin, or we may be lead to consider the spiritual life as purely something individual.

2. At the origin of the journey in the Spirit we can recognize three interlocking initiatives.

The *first* is God's initiative: the initiative of life and salvation in Christ Jesus. (cf. Eph. 1: 3–14) New life is God's gift, by means of Christ, in the Spirit, and it is given us in the Church. It is the grace of purification, of sanctification and of consecration. (cf. 1 Cor. 6:11)

God establishes us as his people. He educates us as his people with the strength of his love. The fullness of grace dwells in God's Son and the new people, and every member of it, participate in it as though they had a personal and living treasure, like the sap that passes from the vine to the branches. 'The love of God has been poured into our hearts by the Holy Spirit which has been given to us.' (Rom. 5:5) God himself in this way is present to his people and he gives life to his sons and daughters from within with the riches of his love. This is the life-giving breath, the energy, which from deep within is the motive force of the Body of Christ and of each and every member.

Each meeting of the founders with Christ and of their followers, chosen by him to build up the Church and to promote life, has its origin in an act of love. It reflects the predilection of the Father for humankind, and of the spouse, the Lord of history for his bride, the Church.

Being aware of this fact is the first aim to be achieved. It must be followed by a profound experience of love, nurtured by the Word and actually seen in the life of the Body of Christ.

The *second* initiative, which is also an aim in this journey of growth, is the experience of being loved by God in his only begotten Son, welcomed by invitation to a relationship of mutual love. 'We have recognized for ourselves and put our faith in the love God has for us.' (John 4:16)

The response to God's gift is faith, a total belonging to him, obedience of faith (cf. Rom. 1:5 16:26) in fully welcoming his Word. It means 'to journey in newness of life'. The Father allows us to participate in the divine *agape*, and our response expressed in dynamic charity is to live in unity, by becoming 'one in Christ.' (cf. Gal. 3:28)

The dialectic of reciprocal love between God and the human race is for Clement of Alexandria the way to the divinization of the Christian. This relationship is achieved in Christ the Lord present among his own. The relationship between God and his people, between Christ and his disciples helps a reciprocal relationship to mature with him and among us in today's Church and world. From this source, following the lamb where ever he goes, much fruit comes to every community and individual in the Church.

This mutual relationship is possible because we have been allowed to enter the life of the Trinity in Christ Jesus. In pictures that we can understand, the Master has explained it for us in the image of 'the vine and the branches' (cf. John 15:1ff); speaking to the Father in his paschal prayer he spoke in the culmination of truth, 'May they all be one, just as, Father, you are in me and I am in you'. (John 17:21)

The conviction that these facts explain both the identity of the Christian and of us religious, and that they are perfectly down to earth and normal, motivates many young people. They discover there, as we adults do too, a vitality from which the world cannot but benefit. The world 'cannot but act in the same way' affirmed Paul VI referring to the witness of men and women religious. (cf. ET 3)

The journey in the Spirit sets out from this mutual relationship with God and among ourselves. We, in virtue of our religious consecration are its 'sign' (cf. 'Elementi Essenziali' 5; LG 44). The journey progresses according to the dynamic of radical love for God and of mutual love among us, his disciples; love in Christ becomes the 'principle of transformation' and of maturity of both the individual and society (cf. GS:38).

It could not be different given our condition as sons and daughters in the Son, and members of the living Church, ikon of the Trinity.

The journey of growth of the individual, and community united in his name, thus becomes both substantial and practical; all aspects of human life are included and it opens new perspectives for apostolic activity in today's world. We need this approach to be able to offer our society the values that change hearts of stone into hearts of flesh where God may live; for our society is fragmented despite the richness of its achievements and its high aspirations.

In the Spirit we turn back to God from the depth of our being as a son turns to his father (cf. Gal. 4:6). Love is mutual and becomes communion by his gift which, in the death of Christ, has destroyed every barrier and conquered the evil one.

Equally, in the Spirit, we now love our brothers and sisters with the very same love with which the Father loves his Son and each of us (cf. John 17:26). The love between each other is a sharing in the communion of love between Father and Son (cf. John 5:19; 17:26; 1 John 4:16). This is the life which creates the climate of Christian and religious community, which promotes the growth of each and of all the members according to particular vocations and tasks in the community. It is both the fundamental law of growth and establishes the 'good' soil (cf. Matt. 13:23) when the Word is welcomed, bread is broken, in fidelity to prayer and the teaching of the Apostles. The dynamic of growth follows the rhythms of participating in the mysteries of Christ if we let ourselves be guided by the instruction of the Church. Through her liturgy, celebrated in community, she progressively inserts us into the death and resurrection of Jesus into his saving journey; and she forms the members of the community into 'living stones' in the building of the kingdom. Frailties, trials, weaknesses do no harm. They invite us to constant vigilance to commit ourselves to an ascetical life in which charity is both life-giving and gives us light to see. So we are perfected as a pilgrim people.

In the Spirit, finally, we can say to the Father who has opened us up in heart and mind to the needs of our brothers and sisters and all humankind: 'Here am I, send me' (Isa. 6:8). As members of the Body of Christ and of the family of the founder, we can make our contribution to form the whole of humankind into the family of God. By means of the Spirit, along this journey of personal and collective growth, the Father little by little leads us to understand 'what no eye has seen, what no ear has heard, what the mind of man cannot visualize' (cf. 1 Cor. 2 – 9:10). In Christ Jesus these things belong to us. They are a reality, not a dream. They are the possession of a simple heart in whom living faith and passionate charity open up ever new horizons of communion, brotherhood and mission.

Such realities are hidden from the wise of the earth but they bring a song to the heart of those who are open in humility and trust, as Mary was, to the action of the Spirit in the community, in themselves and in the world.

There is a *third* initiative which is a source and foundation stone of the dynamic of growth in Christ and in the Church. It is the experience of the spirit of the founders. It is worth while speaking of that experience of Christ, by the work of the Holy Spirit, which constitutes the heart of the charism of the founder, and is the patrimony of the life of the institute. Here also, at the origins, there is an experience of a mysterious and passionate love of God, the reciprocal love with Christ the Lord which emerges from a personal call. But there is another datum: the call is not made to Francis alone, Ignatius alone, or Don Bosco alone, and so on. It is made to each of them, and to as many called to build the family of the Founder. 'A whole group is called to be present and to operate in it precisely as a community of persons.' (F. Ciardi)

This is an important and significant datum for the role of religious life in the Church in its 'evangelical memory' (G.-C. Guy).[1] It is worth saying that the dynamic of growth in the Spirit involves a journey which is at the same time personal and communitarian. It is undertaken together with our brothers and sisters, both as members of the ecclesial community and of the religious community; and it is a journey that reveals both the uniqueness of every person in Christ, and is an epiphany of the Risen One and of the Church, in the unity of the members together.

These riches permeate the journey of growth and indicate its evangelical value. This is also why a simple gesture or step taken in the obedience of faith (as for Mary) acquires value as an ecclesial and prophetic sign: it is a mediation of Christ's life.

3. As we go on talking of the profound elements of our identity and the sources of life from which we are drawn, a determining fact stands out clearly at the end of the maturing of individuals and communities. After becoming 'one in Christ', as Paul writes to the Galatians, after becoming the people of God, established in unity and capable of living in communion, we become ourselves only in so far as we know how to project and live communion in daily life, as it comes to us in each present moment.[2] The present moment is the living synthesis of history and openness to the future; and it is where we face God's will, and our brothers and sisters. So the itinerary becomes clear and organic while it takes on its own special form ever more fully, according to God's plan for each person in the Church.

In our age when the person is so much emphasized by society, the spiritual life incorporates the dimension of man and of woman growing in the following of Christ under the guidance of the Spirit. This growth is both into unity and communion, and into their personal uniqueness as individuals. This comes partly from the return to the sources, partly from the values acquired through biblical and anthropological reflections, partly through the growing experience of the Church.

In our age when solidarity, and the discovery of being complementary to each other, become cultural elements of high priority, the spiritual life is making rediscoveries. It proposes growth in Christ not in glorious isolation, but as members of the ecclesial communion, as disciples united in the name of the Lord, and participating in the charism of one's particular founder.

In our age of secularism when the sacred is being set aside, the spiritual life is seen as an evangelical journey towards the perfection of charity available for all: the young, adults, those under vows, members of families ... Journeys that are a celebration of life lived daily, in attentive service of our brothers and sisters, in dialogue with every person of good will, and in loving welcome of every suffering and every longing.

Finally in our age of renewal in the Church, an age of surprising creativity of the Spirit (cf. EN 75), the spiritual life concentrates on the vital and constitutive realities of the mystery of Christ and of the Church. This is a mystery both of communion and of the Church as the universal sacrament of salvation. The Church is an increasing and visible expression of unity and so it fulfils its mission. The rediscovery both of the Fathers of the Church and of the great spiritual teachers and of the mystics, also of the schools of spirituality, and particularly in our age, the flowering of the movements, all work together in supporting the Christian and each person to live out his or her own vocation, and to operate with maturity and responsibility in daily life in both Church and world.

The Focolare Movement has its part to play in this. It is also contributing to holiness and charity. It has witnessed the flowering of desert places, and now in the glorious springtime of a new epoch emerging for the year two thousand, Mary is actively present as a mother. She leads us ahead as the one who 'precedes' in the Church in this her journey in the history of humankind. (cf. RM 45–49).

II The Stages of the journey of growth in the Spirit

1. We would now like to penetrate more fully into the dynamic of the growth of our life in the Spirit.

It is a delicate and difficult task. The various religious families have in fact their own spiritual traditions. For the most part the great schools of Christian spirituality are identified with religious life; or religious orders have at least been enriched by them in the development of the charism from their initial foundation.[3] All of them express the multiform riches of the mystery of Christ and reveal him to the world in diverse historical, social and cultural situations. As they develop, in harmony with the historic journey of the Church, the Ikon of the Trinity, all of these spiritual traditions become more clearly a part of the 'sovereign plan', and 'Christ's supreme plan', which is unity (cf. John 17:21–23). Unity is the Father's gift, the constitutive reality of the people of God in Christ the Lord, the 'focal point' of Christian Life.[4]

2. On this background we would like to make clear some objective principles, regarding the presence of Mary as both figure and model for the Church.

Every journey in the Spirit is an itinerary of faith or better a 'pilgrimage of faith'. It is about both the entire Church as the body of Christ or pilgrim people, and each of its members; and we are concerned in particular about religious, for the specific task their vocation gives them in ecclesial life.

Lumen Gentium follows the Fathers of the Church and puts forward Mary as the model of perfection for the Church. It also has a section on those of us who embrace religious life, that is those who embrace the form of life which the Word made flesh chose for himself and proposes for his own close followers, and which Mary herself embraced (cf. LG 44–46). 'Mary is a model of the Church in the matter of faith, charity, and perfect union with Christ'. (LG 63). She is the model of that motherly love which should animate those in the apostolic missionary work of the Church who co-operate in the regeneration of humankind (cf. LG 65). In her response of faith and in her constant disposition to the call of the Spirit, she is the model to follow in the daily round of life.

John Paul II writes in *Redemptoris Mater* her ' . . . going before as a figure or model . . . her exceptional pilgrimage of faith represents a constant point of reference for the Church, for individuals and for communities, for peoples and nations, and in a sense for all humanity' (RM 5 – 6).

The Marian dimension characterizes the Church as do the Apostolic and Petrine dimensions. The Pope even underlined this in his recent talk to the Cardinals and prelates of the Roman Curia.[5]

The intimate link that unites the Mother of God to Christ and to the Church clarifies the itinerary of Mary not only as a personal reality but as an event which involves the entire people of God. Her journey is the journey of the Church. The collective character of growth in the Spirit thus becomes more clear. The people of God fulfils in history its journey of discipleship, and of the perfection in charity, until it attains full maturity in Christ (cf. Eph. 4:13). In God's plan, salvation and sanctification are not simply individual facts, each disconnected from the other, without any link. God has willed to establish us as 'a people' (LG 9). It is worth saying that as the Body of Christ animated by the Holy Spirit, we are committed to love God with all our heart, soul, mind and strength (cf. Matt. 12:30), and to love each other as Christ has loved us (cf. John 15:12). The link that unites all the members is the new commandment; it is the very Spirit of Christ himself who is working in everybody. The special feature of the pilgrimage of faith of the Christian is that it sets out from these living realities: reciprocal love both with Christ the Lord and among us, his disciples and brothers and sisters. We as religious are called to witness and be signs of these things, living and deepening them continually in our community and personal life. Indeed the structures of religious life should be, by their nature, a public witness of the primacy of God, of brotherly and sisterly communion, and of being missionaries. We are called to 'go before' in the Church, like Mary. As has been God's teaching throughout history, the Spirit, (and Christ the head wills this) introduces new gifts into the tissue of the Church, both to promote the constant renewal of religious life and to strengthen the links of the Body of Christ, and to give life to its functions and activities (cf. MR 5).

Perhaps in Western culture it is difficult to assume a mentality 'as a people' and to have the awareness of being a member of a living organism, the Church. We can have the impression, or the fear, that the individual will lose his or her own freedom or originality, or that in practice it means opening the doors to conformity, or to a mortifying dependence. Perhaps also for this reason Pope Paul VI used to emphasize the necessity 'of a teaching, of a formation that makes us used to thinking and acting as parts of the other, as children and brothers and sisters of this ecclesial communion.'[6]

3. In the itinerary of growth in the Spirit, in the light of the experience of Mary we can distinguish three fundamental moments or phases. We can relate them to the process of initial formation, from preparation for the novitiate to final profession; and they are present in different ways and to a different extent in the various phases of adult life up to the final consummation of the last call.

From the Annunciation to the meeting with Simeon in the Temple

4. When we meditate on Mary the mother of Jesus and of the Church, in order to understand from her experience the meaning of vocation, the laws of life and of mission, our gaze stops at the mystery of the Annunciation (cf. Luke 1: 26 – 38). The young girl of Nazareth is called by name. She is 'full of grace', and she encounters the passionate love of God for his people: 'My heart within me is overwhelmed, fever grips my inmost being' (Hos. 11:18). 'That is why I yearn for him' (Jer. 31:20, cf. Isa. 49: 14 – 15). She must have felt an overwhelming love for God, which had been nourished in her by participating in the history of his people. She had celebrated with that people the memorial of the covenant, and the covenant was now very close to her. By meditating and appreciating in herself the promises made to Abraham, also the law of the covenant and the word of the prophets, Mary had grown 'into the affairs of God'. So almost with a connatural sharing in the work of the Holy Spirit, 'she understood' from deep within herself the ineffable vibrations of his love, and this love overwhelmed her so she replies: 'Behold I am the handmaid of the Lord, let it be done to me according to thy word.' Mary recognizes and ratifies

the covenant of God with his people, and she involves the people of God in fulfilling the plan of salvation. She is the daughter of Sion, and she involves God's people by giving flesh to the Word, and by offering the fruit of her womb, the son of David, as a pleasing offering to God. In her 'yes' Mary shows she is united to God in that love with which he loves his people, the world, and all men and women in the world.

The whole life of Mary from then on is lived in relationship with Jesus according to the Father's plan. Its greatness lies in God's choice who wants her to share in a unique way in the plan of salvation by her motherly mediation. Her greatness lies in her reply of faith. She believes. She welcomes the gift that God makes her of himself, and she replies by giving herself wholly to him. All her life unfolds in this mysterious, fascinating and unforseen relationship, and in the continual obedience of faith, which will open her to an ever more profound knowledge of her Son and of the Father who has sent him. She will grow to understand more fully the dimension of the love of God for her, for his people, for the whole of humankind.

5. The Annunciation is the departure point from which Mary begins her new itinerary towards God, her 'pilgrimage' of faith, the paschal journey from Old Testament faith to the faith of Jesus, the Son of the most high. The meeting with Elizabeth when she communicated the gift she has received is a confirmation, thanksgiving and proclamation of her faith: 'Blessed is she who has believed!' It is a further recognition of the mystery of the Father's love. It is praise for the sanctifying fruits in John the Baptist and in Elizabeth of the presence of the Lord in her womb. The Visitation indicates a delicate and active charity which contemplates the wonder of God in a moment of communion between two people. It is the moment of a prophetic joyful canticle. It is a limpid announcement of the fruits of the loving and astonishing presence of the love of the Father in Christ poured out onto the whole of humankind.

Mary grows in understanding the mystery both of the Son and of the Father's love, as she makes more and more new discoveries, such as the events of Bethlehem, with the birth of her son, the exultation of the angels and shepherds, and later at the meeting with Simeon. The Son of the most high, he who will be called holy and will sit on the throne of David, is also the light for the nations and a sign of contradiction. Simeon's words confirm the truth of the Annunciation, but they shed new light on the announcement that Mary heard from the angel. They tell her 'the actual historical situation in which the Son is to accomplish his mission; namely, in misunderstanding and sorrow.' While this announcement on the one hand confirms the faith of Mary in the accomplishment of the promises, on the other hand 'it . . . reveals to her that she will have to live her obedience of faith in suffering, at the side of the suffering Saviour, and that her motherhood will be mysterious and sorrowful' (RM 16).

We can observe from the Annunciation to the meeting with Simeon in the Temple, the first great phase in Mary's life which encloses the whole mystery of her role in the salvific mission of the Son, and her place as mother in the Church and of humankind.

6. What about us? How does this journey help us to understand the fundamental moments of our itinerary of growth in Christ? How does it make us attentive to the *kairòs* – that is those unique moments when the Lord visits each person, or when he comes to visit us as communities or religious families? Perhaps we can gather a few indications which will throw light on our path.

(a) A precious and fundamental moment is the period of time that comes before the Annunciation. Mary came prepared for that meeting at Nazareth. God had educated her in living the life of her own people, feeding herself on the word, faithful to the law and to prayer, loving God with all her heart and her neighbour as herself. The pattern is the same, both for us older religious and for the young men and women whom the Lord calls to a life of consecration. Maturing in the life of faith, in docility to the Spirit, putting the word into practice, celebrating the sacraments, journeying together with our brothers and sisters, growing in mutual love, being attentive to the teaching of the Apostles and to the Church's magisterium, serving the poor: all of this constitutes a precious school in which little by little we grow as persons into human and Christian fullness. The Spirit who knows God's plans, prepares us for the event that changes our whole life, as for Mary at Nazareth. Our part is to welcome the gift God makes of himself to us, in the obedience of faith. He calls us by name, and our response should be freely and completely to abandon ourselves to him. This meeting occurs in the simplest of ordinary ways, according to the culture of each time and place. Every itinerary is down to earth, circumscribed, clothed in the particular details of the person and their culture. The journey is that of a pilgrim people in history. It knows weaknesses, moments of tiredness, sin and doubt. It knows that the love of God and of Mary goes before it. It knows the effort necessary for 'learning about everything'; it knows how much care we need in protecting the life of the Spirit, how hard it is to learn 'how to lose' and to take up the cross each day. But this is precisely the way it completes its journey, guided by the Spirit of Christ. It overcomes every obstacle and the barriers of darkness with the strength of faith, believing in him and gratefully entrusting itself to him. This faith consists in doing his will where we are, together with our brothers and sisters with whom we share our ideals and choices, in the life of the world as it is, and among our own people.

(b) There is a second fundamental and decisive moment. Like Mary who replied 'yes' to the Lord's call, the nuptial Amen, a new reality flowers in the person. Love that is reciprocal is always fruitful. With the 'yes' something happens that changes the person. Life takes a qualitative leap. This growing quality of life indeed gives witness to Christ. Even if the journey beforehand had been one of fidelity and commitment, it now acquires a different style. It becomes that of following with an undivided heart and belonging solely to God. For Francis of Assisi the kiss when meeting the leper was a decisive option for Christ. He entered God's plan for him as he discovered it day by day in doing his will (i.e., the obedience of faith). For Ignatius, the period at Manresa where the Lord of history awaited him, changed his existence. There in that place and during that long period of time, he learnt to know him, and to know his plan of love. The love of the Father and the Son conquered him, and it was impossible for him not to communicate the fire that burned in him to others, to conquer them for the Lord and build with them. For my founder (Eugene de Mazenod) it was on Good Friday when the lamentations of Jeremiah were sung in the choir of Aix Cathedral. It felt as though he heard the 'groans' of the spouse of Christ who was calling him 'with a loud voice'. Something like this happens for each founder. There is a particular moment of God which marks a change in life. So it is for us, each in our own way, for us singly, for us as a family of our founder or as a group united in his name. What counts is not the small or great event, or whether the mediation is extraordinary or simple: but that there, in that place, at that moment I have met him, I have known him, and I have left my nets to follow him.

The itinerary and the journey in the Spirit develops from then onwards according to this gift: the 'come and follow me of men and women religious'. This reveals to us our true name and our position in the Church; it allows us to enter and to be ever more involved in the Father's plan of salvation. Little by little we begin to read reality with a new eye, as if a new light at last let us see within. The word of God, our daily support, digs within and carves 'in letters of fire' the truths that it communicates. The present acquires value as the meeting place with God, and it is the practical expression of our love for him and our brothers and sisters. 'I will always find someone to serve in order to serve you'. 'I was hungry and you gave me food, I was thirsty and you gave me drink'. The poor attract us. Go with them and suffer with them. Learn from them because they are a 'mediation' of the Father for each person and for the religious family.

With our brothers and sisters who share the same ideal we commit ourselves to journey with readiness in chastity, poverty and obedience, loving God and our neighbour. We learn to forgive each other in order to journey with greater intensity. We do not want to dwell on the mistakes which can fill our day in most unusual ways. Instead we are able to gaze at him who transforms every situation with the irresistable force of love; a redemptive love. Every act of forgiveness is redemptive love, which rebuilds union with God and with others according to his plan.

We are ready to learn to appreciate the value of mutual charity and to appreciate its fruits. An intense life of mutual charity among members of the community opens us up to the gift of the Lord's presence there, promised to those who are united in his name (cf. Matt. 18:20). We could call this an experience of ecclesial communion, being Church, in which the Lord is present; being a living cell of the Church. He who has called us by name and lives in us, now reveals to us his family, the Church; it is revealed as it lives, works, prays, suffers, is renewed and grows. He communicates to us his passion for the world's salvation. Together with him present in the community (cf. PC 15) we welcome the word, break bread, pray to the Father, move among the people to help set up the kingdom. The community will now seem to be complete because the body has a head and everyone has the same desire: to fulfil the works of the Father. We are talking here of a way of life. Our experience already gained in formation tells us how important these growth points are, especially if they happen regularly in the life of the young generation and for us adults. They give something extra to life; they help us to understand the Church better, as a communion and universal sacrament of salvation. Also if later we do have to live on our own, we feel the Church within ourselves; we are a part of a living organism and an expression of all, in virtue of the communion of saints.

(c) The journey will continue with the help of our brothers and sisters, and in an ever more practical and refined charity. The intention and the will are directed ever more constantly to Him. We learn to know him like Mary, living the life of our own people, in prayer, in studying, in work, in listening to the word which the Church proclaims to us in the eucharistic celebration.

So we will arrive at another precious and important moment in our formation: the meeting with our Simeon in the temple; i.e., the place of God's presence: in prayer, in community life, in the Word, in our brothers and sisters,

190

in suffering. He will reveal to us other faces of the Lord who has called us; and new aspects of Mary. He reveals Jesus, a sign of contradiction, and the bond Mary had with her suffering son. We are asked to meet him 'face to face'. This is always happening in our daily journey which takes us into the life of society today. A new horizon is opened up for us, the cross. The journey is a more difficult one, and it becomes more authentic. Nobody can escape this new meeting with the love of God that he gives us, and which calls us anew into suffering. Our response of faith and love will be to choose him crucified, the wisdom of God and source of life.

This is the narrow door, beyond which we will glimpse new horizons of light and life. At the same time we will be aware that we are 'the voice of every created thing'. Our existence is for them: 'Here I am, send me.'

7. The daily awarenes of how strong secularism is, and the toxic atmosphere of consumerism can damage the vision of faith, leading it to be cast aside, and allowing other itineraries pride of place. This is when the trial can become harder, because others, and even our own brothers or sisters in religious life, may not understand. Mutual help with those who do understand, brotherly or sisterly communion in authentic charity, feeding on solid food, such as God's Word, reconciliation and the constant effort to make our community a family of God which enjoys his presence, not only make us vigilant and attentive, but lead us to love every suffering, to present ourselves to others with the transparency of Mary, and to offer to each person a breathing space, life, the Good News. We realize that 'the measure of charity is to be without measure' (Paul VI). 'Love each other as I have loved you' (John 13:14).

Eventually we will understand that the key for the trans-formation of humankind and the world is to be found in the cross of Christ Jesus, where we can see the fullness of love and the way to unity. We will probably finally understand through meeting somebody, or through some small event: or even in some very hard turn of events in our life. We will then know the deep roots that are needed for authentic communion with our brothers and sisters.

Advancing along this path, guided by the Word, with 'heartfelt effort', we take on ourselves as he did, the world's sufferings today: the immense poverty, the heartrending divisions, every trouble of our brothers or sisters. They are all ours. We are made for them.

Running along this road faithfully, the moment comes when we feel we are called to love everybody with his measure, which is the cross. A new decision springs up for us from this: 'I do not know anyone save Christ, and Christ crucified'. I carry in myself 'his wounds' and those of his body the Church.

In both initial and permanent formation, these experiences confirm the vocation and journey undertaken in religious life, individually, and in our own institute. They are a great help in recognizing the validity of this journey, and of discovering the dynamic laws of growth in the Spirit. Also the commitment to follow Christ joyfully, and in union with our brothers and sisters in the community influences others, and so the apostolate itself is more fruitful (PC 15). Another confirmation is found in the increasingly joyful inter-congregational meetings which take place. Getting to know each other, and the exchange of personal experiences, allows us personally to touch God's action and his personal love for each person. These are unique moments of formation, also because they open us up to the Church ever more fully. We feel we are a pilgrim people, and we can be continuously enriched by communion with both ancient and modern charisms of the Spirit in the Church, and in the complementary nature of different forms of the apostolate.

Nazareth

8. What can happen now for the religious in his or her journey of growth is the same for any disciple or indeed any religious community: a new phase of life opens which naturally follows the previous one. In fact the proceeding journey has established the foundations for it. These foundations are consolidated and developed according to God's plan for each person. The individual and the community have

attained enough maturity to enter the heart of the spiritual experience. They have been open, in trusting faith, to the Master and to the experience of communion with him. On the basis of love the deepest link can now develop with Christ and with the Church. The conditions have been achieved for an experience that allows individuals or communities to be worthy to discern the action of the Spirit, to fulfil the works of the Father, to realize God's plans, and to be of service to our brothers and sisters according to the charism of the founder. A 'school' following the Lord might be the best description of this stage, with an itinerary tending towards the perfection of charity; and its reference point is the hidden life of Nazareth.

Among the aspects of this phase of the journey are: carefully protecting the gift of faith; the trials that help the consolidation and growth of life in Christ and the Church; and the new, or the 'second conversion'.

Protecting the gift of faith

9. Love demands its first commitment deep within us to be to protect carefully the gift received, abandoning ourselves to God in faith. What can happen is that as the implications of living the Gospel are appreciated by others, as others get to know us, and see our stand on pastoral, ecclesial or civil matters, this gift of faith is not always welcomed. It may even be rejected by those for whom we offer our lives, or to whom we are linked by bonds of friendship, blood or common work. We are faced with the burden of the misunderstanding of the choice of religious life and of our ideals. We can feel rejected or put aside because of our radical choice of Christ. There might also be intimate sufferings. They are often generated by secularism, or by cultural conditioning of various kinds, which seem to poison the values we uphold in ourselves, and our brotherly or sisterly style of life, the freshness of faith or Gospel ideals.

To protect the gift of faith is not an escape. It means living more intensely with Jesus, in faith and love, by giving our life in charity to all. To protect means refining our life of prayer, and refining the reciprocal relationships in the community. It is to love in a more practical way, always being the first to love. It means facing up to ourselves in order to discern God's will and his ways; it means valuing all that is positive in each person, even in the one who no longer understands us. To protect means knowing how to wait for the moment of God, with attentive love.

All this strengthens us, and leads us to reflect on Mary and Joseph. They had to leave home and go into exile in Egypt, where they lived a full life with their son, awaiting God's hour to return among their own people.

This experience also helps us to understand that living in situations of conflict and rejection is a part of the prophetic dimension of religious life, which is a 'sign of contradiction'. This will be all the more evident according to the transparency of our witness to the Gospel and our joyful fidelity to Christ. The signs that such conflicts are not 'of flesh and blood' are the fruits of the Spirit (cf. Gal. 5:22).

Trials

10. The individual can experience the first true spiritual trials which are the great school of maturing of the new self, as the history of the people of God attests. That history is the story of salvation.

At a certain moment of the journey, our enthusiasm, our interior commitment, joy and attraction for prayer, self sacrifice and life in community may seem to disappear. Everything can become dark. In their place enters dryness, tiredness, confusion, interior weariness . . . Doubts of faith come back; we wonder whether the initial choice was the right one. Temptations and struggle may afflict us. Even the relationships of communion, brotherhood or sisterhood seem to mean nothing with members of our own community, with whom we had begun the journey together in the Lord's name. The very presence of the Lord in the community can seem to disappear. The religious family seems a long way away. All efforts at renewal, and the commitment to journey on, or to evangelization seem inconsistent, or empty of value. We can have 'the sensation of losing everything: our person, and life past, present and future. All meaning and light, taste and will for the religious life, courage for a re-start are not there.'[7]

All of us have lived through these moments, or have accompanied our brothers and sisters in this trial on their journey. We know the amount of suffering and the number of graces contained there. This is the time when we mature in our depth as religious, at the heart of our being, in the light of the values in the following of the chaste, poor and obedient Christ. His word penetrates to the living heart of our being, like a two edged sword.

This trial touches each person's humanity, their style of life, their speaking and acting, their reference points, their relationships, the preceeding journey. The value of everything is weighed up: not to make judgements on things, but so that we build on the rock, and that our person may flower according to God's plan, and life may become full, beautiful and renewed.

In this period we can learn how to know both God and ourselves better, his plan, the Church and the world. We can learn that all is God's gift, without any merit of our own. We can learn to distinguish how much is due to him, and how little is the result of flesh and blood. We can learn how to ask humbly with the tenacious simplicity of love, that God may truly be the unique centre of our existence. We can learn how to recognize his love everywhere, even in what seems absurd to the eye or human mind.

This life unfolds ever more within ourselves and the community, and we are able to share it with others. Others are welcomed as gifts for us, persons with their own talents.

Our life of union with God is thus consolidated. We can grow in inner harmony and learn what has more value and what has less, and our motives can become constantly more pure. We can realize the value that a community 'united in his name' has for the Church and evangelization.[8] As this becomes more important, any attitude of dependency, or of efforts based on our emotions, give way to a practical, concrete, initiating and disinterested love, which does not expect anything from others, but is always giving.

Those trials do not necessarily lead to compromise. They can consolidate and open us up. Each person can discover and experience that the fulfilment of man or woman and a religious community resides in the sharing in the life of God in Christ Jesus. We can become certain that the life of a person becomes so much more human and harmonious in so far as he or she is 'a spiritual person'; i.e., in so far as the divine life enters his or her humanity and is grafted onto Christ.

Basically the growth journey of the person consecrated to God in this powerful school is substantiated, and guided, by all that forms it into the 'living nucleus' of life in Christ and of the charism, of the founder. This is why Mary is put before us as a model and guide during those long years at Nazareth in her mysterious relationship with her son. John Paul II writes in Redemptoris Mater:

She 'who believed that there would be a fulfilment of what was spoken to her by the Lord' (Luke 1:45) lives the reality of these words day by day. And daily at her side is the Son to whom 'she gave the name Jesus'; ... Mary knows that he who bears the name Jesus has been called by an angel 'the Son of the most high'. (cf. Luke 1:32) Mary knows she has conceived and given birth to him 'without having a husband', by the power of the Holy Spirit, by the power of the most high who overshadowed her (cf. Luke 1:35), ... Mary knows that the Son to whom she gave birth in a virginal manner is precisely that 'holy one', the Son of God, of whom the angel spoke to her ... she his mother is in contact with the truth about her Son only in faith and through faith ... (she) continues to believe, day after day amidst all the trials and the adversities of Jesus' infancy and then during the years of the hidden life in Nazareth, where 'he was obedient to them.' (Luke 2:51) ... A sort of 'night of faith' ... a kind of veil through which one has to draw near to the invisible one, and to live in intimacy with the mystery. Even his mother, to whom had been revealed most completely the mystery of his divine sonship, 'did not understand' the saying that he spoke to her and Joseph after finding him again in the Temple. 'Did you not know that I must be about my father's business?' (Luke 2:48 – 50) Truly the blessing pronounced by

Elizabeth during the visitation 'Blessed is she who has believed' is fulfilled in her day by day.[1] (RM 17)

At this school of faith which functions by means of charity (Gal. 5:6) the indentity of the religious and the community marked with the presence of Christ becomes more evident. 'Christ lives in me' affirms Paul writing to Galatians (5:6); 'Christ is our life' he declares in the letter to the Colossians (3:4).

The Second Conversion

11. Our awareness of God's love and this more intimate union with him is a vital background to a new call deep within each person. He calls you anew by name. You recognize him. You choose him again with the help of grace which urges us on. You follow him in a peace and joy that you never dreamed of and which nothing can disturb. Your whole person is projected into Christ Jesus, crucified and risen. The design of the Father in Christ becomes now your own personal project, deep in the heart. In itself this is a strong and fruitful witness in your religious order, in the Church and in society.

Faith is thus expressed in a living, dynamic charity which is increasingly active and fruitful. We find that we submit more quickly and smoothly to the Holy Spirit and to God's will. The same occurs because of the new relationship with Christ and him crucified: we give to God all our being, our person, our affections, intelligence, our talents and activities.

Christ, the Spirit of Christ, and the call by name to 'come and follow me' are immeasurably valuable gifts received by us from the Father. They do not, however, fall on immaculate soil, as in Mary. Rather they fall on soil where pride, egoism, sensuality, weaknesses and attachments are intrinsic; all of these can imprison our freedom as children of God and harden the heart. Or again, for reasons such as searching for the perfection of charity, for fraternal communion, or for the work of the apostolate, we can

197

have mixed motives at the heart of our selves: and these are often motives which give priority to our own interest rather than God's interest, that follow our plans and our ways rather than his. The Father who is in heaven and who thinks of the lilies of the field and of the birds in the air, knows all that we need to flower as new creatures, to be transparent images of his only Son. He leads us through the 'narrow door' to the pastures of life. The narrow door is also the hidden life of silence, as at Nazareth, with the self-renunciations and self-sacrifices that are part of it. But it is at this point that union with God is strengthened and faith becomes vibrant. We find that a feel for the Church develops, which leads us to the service of our brothers and sisters so that the Bride of Christ may express all her holiness and achieve unity 'so that the world may believe' (cf. John 17:21).

'Woman, behold your Son' (John 19:26)

12. I do not wish to prolong this discussion. Yet I really must underline again that these phases in growth in the Spirit, with Mary present to us in her pilgrimage of faith as our model, are not only for the individual. Certainly each individual is called to journey on his or her own road, which cannot be repeated by others. But these phases are also lived by communities 'united in the name of the Lord' (cf. PC 15), by religious families precisely through sharing the 'spiritual experience' of the founder; and these are called to develop and deepen that 'spiritual experience' with their own life in Christ in the Church (cf. MR11).

It would certainly be illuminating and enriching to read the history of our institutes and of religious life from the viewpoint of their unity with the entire Church. It would mean a study of the journey lived in the Spirit in the Church, which is the body of Christ as it is growing and changing. But we would need first of all to have a prolonged experience of spiritual life in communion with others, to be able to possess 'co-naturally' the criteria to read, and to know how to discern, the signs of God's action and his teaching.

13. The 'second conversion' opens a new phase in life. It is the period when our spiritual maturity is shown in the works we do, in the construction of our own religious family and community, in our apostolic commitment, and in the progress of our own formation, for the achievement of the aims of our own institute, and for the needs of the Church. When, like Mary who followed Jesus in his public life, we graciously allow the Spirit to lead us, we communicate the life which is Christ, in preference for the poor, and those far away from God. We commit ourselves to develop communities which can become 'living' centres, rich in humanity, universal, wide and welcoming, and pregnant with his presence; prayer centres, schools of the Word of God, where we can have an authentic divine experience (cf. DCVR 15), and where we can learn to be of service to everybody with respect for them and for their freedom; where new generations can be formed as disciples of Christ, each according to his or her own vocation; from where we can set out to journey with our founders on the roads of the world of today, and to make a neighbour of every person we meet, like the Lord, who gave life that we might have life.

14. The journey in the obedience of faith and in active charity opens out onto a more profound and precious aim. It is the culmination of the life of Mary. Living with her means to take part with her in the 'hour' of Jesus: the hour of suffering, of separation, of death and of life.

> At the foot of the cross Mary shares through faith in the shocking mystery of this self-emptying ... (who) precisely on Golgotha 'humbled himself and became obedient unto death, even death on a cross' (cf. Phil 2:5 –8). This is perhaps the deepest 'kenosis' of faith in human history. (RM 18)

And Mary became the mother of the Church and of the whole of humankind through the work of the Spirit: 'Woman, behold your son' (John 19:26).
The result of Christ's love for the Father and for human-

kind is the motherly presence of Mary who continues to show herself in the Church, in our religious families and in the life of all, who, like her 'have believed' in Jesus. They are following him like Mary, to be of service to the Church in this most delicate moment of history, our present age. A new epoch has opened, made fruitful by the Spirit in which Mary is present who unites everybody around her Son, so that the human family may depose the works of evil and enjoy the gifts of life.

In Mary's school we learn that the desert will flower only through the strength of love. The Marian profile in the Church, as bride and mother, is a whole style of life, which includes service, and is a particular kind of presence in the world.

15. Following the Lord who has called us by name, and has gathered us together puts before us this challenge at all the various stages of our life, so that we can live like Mary and fully be fathers and mothers in the Spirit. Our founders developed into mature sons and daughters of the Church. In their hearts, there dwelt only God and the Church. 'To love God is to love the Church' (Eugene de Mazenod). From now on we too are called to the same high calling as consecrated men and women, whose only treasure is God, and whose only word is the Word.

May Mary, Mother of the Church and of humankind be our teacher and guide.

REFERENCES
1. G.C., Guy, SJ, *La Vie Religieuse memoire evangelique de l'Eglise*, Le Centurion, Paris 1987.
2. To go deeper into this point see 'G. Helewa – E. Ancilli, *La spiritualità cristiana. Fondamenti biblici e sintesi storica*, Teresianum, Roma 1986, Chapter VI: 'Un cuore solo e un'anima sola'. pp. 69–91.
3. cf. *Le grandi Scuole della spiritualità cristiana*, edt. by E. Ancilli, Teresianum, Roma, 1984.
4. Paul VI, Homily on Holy Thursday, 30 March, 1972. Also Paul VI, Homily at the concelebration with the Italian Bishops, 8 June 1974.

5. John Paul II, Talk to the college of cardinals and to the Roman curia, in the Italian edition of the Osservatore Romano, 23/12/1987.

6. Paul VI, talk on 8 June 1966.

7. F. Ruiz OCD, *Crescere in Cristo. La dinamica spirituale. Aspetti personali e communitari,* in AA.VV *Il cammino nello Spirito,* Rogate, Roma, 1986, pp. 36–37.

8. cf. Perfectae Caritatis, no. 15.

VI THE SPIRITUALITY OF THE FOCOLARE MOVEMENT AND RELIGIOUS LIFE

Chiara Lubich

Dear Priests and Brothers, the talk I am about to give deals with two subjects: the spirituality of the Focolare Movement and the religious who live it. Therefore I will try, first of all, to explain our spirituality briefly.

The spirituality of unity

As we all know, a spirituality in the Church is, as Paul VI said, 'the way in which we try to fulfil the ideal of Christian life.'[1] Thus we must illustrate how the members of the Focolare Movement live Christianity.

We will try to discover, as Paul VI suggested, speaking about the spirituality of the Curé d'Ars, "the operative principles, the powerful inspirations, the guide lines . . . "[2] in our spirituality.

This task is extremely difficult because a spirituality in the Church is Christianity. It is evangelical life, the Gospel, even if it is all viewed from a particular angle.

It is a difficult task to explain in a few words the evangelical life that God has been weaving together day by day for over forty years, together with those ideas or inspirations which he gives step by step to the instruments he uses in order to present again to the world the eternal truth of the Good News in a form that is always new and is suited to the needs of the times.

It is quite difficult to pour out in a few pages the infinite riches of a life, of a supernatural life. But having stated this premiss, I too will try to describe some of the ideas that are powerful inspirations and some aspects of our spirituality, as they began to take shape.

Due to a profound rediscovery of the Word of God during the first months of life of our Movement, we were convinced that our spirituality was simply to live the Gospel, the Gospel which was for everyone, the Gospel as it has always been. God was emphasizing in our heart, unbeknown to us, some of his words which were becoming the powerful inspiring ideas, the lines with which a new spirituality was being formed.

God Love

The inspiring spark, as Pope John Paul II defined it,[3] the first idea, was a renewed revelation of God as Love. Because of the war, everything which could have been the ideal of our life crumbled, and from on high came the invitation to make God the reason of our existence, God who was then manifesting himself as Love.

What a change this truth brought into our lives in those early days of the Movement once it has been understood through a gift from God in a completely new way. It still brings about this change today in those who succeed in grasping it.

The Christian life that we led before this new understanding even though enriched by a solid faith and by integrity in its practice, appeared to be overshadowed by a feeling of being orphans. Now everything was new. God was Love. And because God was love, he was a Father. Our heart which had lived almost in the exile of the night of life, opened out towards God who loved us, who thought of everything, who counted even the hairs on our head.

The joyful and painful circumstances of our life acquired a totally new meaning: everything had been forseen by God. Nothing could frighten us anymore. We felt we were the object of his love: we 'have been taken up into God's hand'.

This is a faith which is an exalting faith, a faith which fortifies. It is a faith which makes people cry the first few times they experience it. It is a gift of God. Whoever finds it and accepts it, takes as his own John's words: 'And we have (. . .) believed in love.' (1 John 4:16)

The will of God

It was this faith in the love that God had for us that inspired us to seek out all the ways we could in order to co-operate with God's love by our love. Therefore we tried to follow those words of the Gospel which told us how we could respond with love to God's love. It was at this point that this phrase became like light for us: 'It is not whoever says Lord, Lord who will enter the kingdom of heaven, but whoever does the will of my Father who is in heaven.' (Matt. 7:21)

Therefore it was not love to call upon God in a sentimental way. It was love to fulfil his will. Doing God's will was the great possibility we had to love God. Doing God's will had been the food of Jesus' life, the way he showed his love to the Father.

And still today all the members of the Movement see in carrying out God's will a way to reply to God's love with their love. This doing the will of God does not mean 'resignation' as often is understood by this phrase, but to launch oneself in the greatest divine adventure in which one can be involved. It is the adventure of carrying out not our own limited projects, but of abandoning ourselves to God and of fulfilling the plan which he has for each of his children, a divine plan far beyond our thoughts, a most rich plan.

If we can therefore state that the first powerful inspiring idea of our spirituality is God-Love, we should say that the second is *to do the will of God*. The Holy Spirit, by imprinting this point of our new spirituality in our heart, also taught us right from the start some small, wise rules for carrying it out with maximum results. He taught us to live God's will in the present moment of life since the past is already gone and the future is not yet in our hands: to live it in the present with perfection, and, I would like to say, with solemnity.

The Holy Spirit also enabled us to discover that in doing the will of God all people of whatever vocation, social class, age and race would find a way of reaching holiness. The carrying out of God's will seemed to us like the entrance ticket to holiness for the crowds.

The new commandment

Among the various and varied wills of God, the Spirit then made us concentrate on the love of our neighbour, which is nothing other than the fulfilment of the law. (Rom. 13:8) We had to love our neighbours in order to love God concretely.

One commandment on charity particularly struck us because Jesus called it 'his' and 'new': *the new commandment*: 'This is my commandment, that you love one another as I have loved you. Greater love has no man than this, that a man lay down his life for his friends.' (John 15:12–13)

This commandment that the focolarine[4] sealed with a mutal promise later became the spiritual foundation of the entire Movement. The practice of this commandment lived to the letter has produced and continues to produce extraordinary effects because where there is charity and love, there is God himself.

Whoever begins to live the New Commandment in a radical way notices a qualitative change in his or her own inner life. It becomes enriched with new strength, with ardour, and with the courage required to start again each time that this is necessary. It is not an exaggeration to say that the carrying out of this commandment produces a real conversion.

Not only this, the practising of this new commandment also has an effect on the world around us. It bears witness to Christ. 'By this all men,' Jesus says, 'will know that you are my disciples, if you have love for one another.' (John 13:3) Many people, because they have observed this sort of love among Christians, reach faith in God-Love and change their lives. Others feel a variety of vocations to follow God; through this love graces of every sort overflow.

The presence of Jesus among us

The New Commandment lived in this way in the Movement also establishes the conditions for accomplishing another fundamental point of our spirituality: *the presence of Jesus among us* according to the words: 'Where two or three are gathered together in my name, I am there in their midst.' (Matt. 18:20)

This presence of Christ among Christians united in him is for the Movement the rule of rules, the necessary condition for every other rule. The members of the Movement can do nothing if this presence is not guaranteed. This presence gives meaning to the supernatural family they are called to live and which Jesus has brought on earth for all humanity.

The abandonment of Jesus

Another powerful, inspiring idea of our spirituality, since it is Christianity, could not be but the cross. It is the contemplation and the application in the life of each individual and of the Movement as a whole, of the passion and death of Jesus.

Through a special circumstance God fixed our attention on a particular part of the passion and death: the *abandonment of Jesus,* of Jesus who 'towards the third hour cried out, "My God, my God why have you forsaken me?"' (Matt. 27:46) It is the drama of a God who cries out: 'My God, why have you forsaken me?'

This extraordinarily deep suffering that Jesus experienced as man is an infinite mystery which gives the measure of his love for us. He wanted to take on himself the separation which kept us far from the Father and far from one another. He overcame this extraordinarily deep suffering when he said: *'In manus tuas, Domine, commendo spiritum meum.'* (Luke 23:46)

The Movement has an extremely rich experience with which it shows how all pain, particularly spiritual pain is summed up in this particular suffering of Jesus.

Is not the person in despair perhaps like him, and also

anyone who is alone? Is not the person experiencing spiritual dryness, the one who is disillusioned, the one who has failed, the one who is weak, similar to him? Is not each painful division among brothers and sisters, among Churches, among sections of humanity with contrasting ideologies the image of him? Is not the atheistic and secularized world, which in its decadence is involved in every sort of abberation, the picture of Jesus who loses, so to speak, the sense of God, of Jesus who has, as Paul says, become 'sin' for us?

In loving Jesus Forsaken the Christian finds the motivation and the strength not to flee from these evils, but to face them, to overcome them and to offer in this way his or her own personal remedy for these evils. This then is Jesus Forsaken who manifests himself as the key to unity with God and among human beings, the key to healing every division.

The Word of Life

Another fundamental idea of our spirituality is the Word of God. The alphabet has only a few letters, but if a person does not know them, and does not learn some grammatical rules, he or she will remain illiterate for the whole of his life. The Gospel is a small book but those who do not live the words contained in it remain underdeveloped Christians, so to speak. They give an image of the Church that does not witness to Christ its founder.

The Holy Spirit has suggested to the Movement right from the start a radical re-evangelization of our own way of thinking, of loving, of willing, of living. As it did in the early period of Christianity, the Church values communion with the Word of God just as it values communion with the Body of Christ.

In the Movement there is the conviction that the Word of God is unique, eternal, universal; it is the presence of God. The members of the Movement discover that having communion with the Word makes them free. It purifies them, converts them, brings them comfort and joy, and gives them wisdom. It produces works and discloses vocations. The Word generates Christ in their souls and in the souls of others, but it also calls forth the hatred of the world.

A complete phrase of the Gospel is offered to all the members of the Movement each month, with a short exegetical commentary. We call it the *Word of Life*.

Everyone lives this Word during the day, remaining inwardly illuminated by it, since living the Word means loving God, and it is written: 'I will manifest myself to the person who loves me.' (cf. John 14:21) The light received and the experiences lived are shared so that the ascent to holiness to which the living of the Gospel leads is achieved together.

The Eucharist

Another fundamental point of the Movement is the *Eucharist*. Most of the members of the Movement have spontaneously felt that they should communicate with Jesus in the Eucharist. It has always been our experience. We believe that the charism of our Movement leads them to do this because the Eucharist is essential to the life of unity. Jesus in the Eucharist is indeed the bond of unity, the most powerful factor for full unity. It is through the Eucharist that there comes to be full communion of people with God, and of people with one another. Before asking the father: 'May they all be perfectly one as you Father are in me, and I am in you' (John 17:24) Jesus had instituted the sacrament that made this fully possible.

Mary

Another 'operative principle' is *Mary*. For us, she is the disciple *par excellence*, the perfect Christian, the living Word of God. And the Movement also feels that Mary is its mother, head, and queen.

That is why it is named after Mary. In fact, it was approved under the name of the Work of Mary. Its various meetings are called 'Mariapolis',[5] the participants in these meetings are the 'Mariapolites', its centres are called 'Mariapolis Centres', each of its small cities is called 'a permanent Mariapolis'.

Mary is the model of each member of the Movement in every aspect of his or her life. But in particular this is because while she had the primordial function of being the mother of the physical Christ, the Movement, as we have seen, has the function (which must precede all others) of, as Paul VI would put it, giving birth to Christ spiritually among human beings.

The presence of Christ in the hierarchy

Another fundamental point of the spirituality of the Movement is *the presence of Jesus in the hierarchy* of the Church. The Movement, aside from the faith which makes it believe that Christ is present in his ministers, has a forty-year experience which witnesses this faith.

St Thérèse of Lisieux says that God uses people in the night of this life "in order to hide His adorable presence, but He does not hide Himself to such an extent that He cannot be discovered."[6] This is what we have always experienced. Behind those who have represented the Church for us, we have seen almost with our own eyes, Jesus.

It has been a very powerful experience. We are convinced that for all those who believe and live according to the words, 'He who hears you, hears me' (Luke 10:16) it is not difficult to have the deepest conviction that Christ is in the representatives of God, despite all human weaknesses. The words of the Gospel emphasize this presence. The Fathers of the Church are the defenders of this presence. The saints have always seen things in this way.

Through its solid faith the Movement has always remained perfectly ingrafted into the hierarchy of the Church, seeking to carry out not only its commands, but its desires. We attribute also to this unity, which is in accordance with God's order, the worldwide explosion of the Movement.

The Holy Spirit

And finally, but this is the *dulcis in fundo* (the sweet thing which comes last), another fixed point: *the Holy Spirit*, who has always been present in the Movement right from the first moments when we invited everyone to listen to his voice. The Holy Spirit, the 'unknown' God, but who is very well known by the Movement which only recognizes itself in a typical atmosphere, an atmosphere in which the Holy Spirit is poured out among the faithful united in the name of Jesus. Furthermore, the Movement recognizes itself through those gifts of his which are characteristic of the persons belonging to the Movement, gifts such as unfailing joy, peace, and light.

Here then is something of our spirituality. It has many aspects which we can also find in other spiritualities. Nevertheless it has its own characteristic. Indeed it has a special name: it is called the 'spirituality of unity' because, as I have explained, although it rests on several fundamental points, there is one which is typically of the Movement: *unity*, the fulfilment of which demands our love for Jesus Forsaken.

All the rest (believing in love, loving, the new commandment, the Word of God, the Eucharist, etc.) are aimed at achieving this end. Therefore our spirituality is Christianity viewed from the Testament of Jesus.[7]

The Focolare Movement and religious

Now I will speak about what I have already told some Superiors General: the religious who adhere to the Movement and particularly, the Movement's contribution to religious.

The religious families as a living Gospel

As we know there is one aspect in the Church which is more institutional and another which is more charismatic. With respect to these two aspects of the Church, the Movement, due to its continual contact with the Gospel, has made a two-fold discovery supported by many years of experience.

On one hand it has seen and experienced that in the hierarchy of the Church (which has also come from the Word of Christ; Paul VI would say, as the plant from a seed)[8], in the hierarchy of the Church there is a very special presence of Jesus to enlighten, to guide and to sanctify the Church. On the other hand, with regard to the more charismatic aspect of the Church, the Movement has contemplated the orders, ' congregations and religious families as splendid flower-beds in the magnificent garden of the Church, in which all the virtues have blossomed and continue to blossom.

Indeed if Christ is the Incarnate Word, the Church appeared to us, because of the many charisms given to her by the Spirit, as an incarnate Gospel. (cf. LG 46) Every religious family, although living with entirety and radicality all the Gospel, is also the incarnation of an expression of Jesus, of an event in his life, of one of his sufferings, of one of his words . . .

There are the Franciscans who continue to preach in the world, also with their very lives, 'Blessed are the poor in spirit, for theirs is the kingdom of God.' (Matt. 5:3) There are the Dominicans who, contemplating the Logos, the Word, explain and spread the truth. The Jesuits underline total availability in serving the Church through obedience. The missionary orders fulfill the precept: 'Go and preach the Gospel to all nations' (Mark 16:15). The Carmelites adore God on Mount Tabor, ready to descend in order to preach and to face the passion and death. The families of Saint Vincent de Paul and Saint Camillus de Lellis incarnate the works of mercy, and so forth.

Because of all these charisms which have blossomed throughout the centuries, the Church truly appears as a Gospel spread out in time and space, because the sons and daughters of the holy founders are often present everywhere.

Now, understanding the Church in this way, how could we view the Movement's relationship with all these riches of the Bride of Christ and in particular, what was the relationship between our spirituality and the others?

Since unity is the characteristic of our spirituality, the 'supreme plan'[9] of Christ, as Paul VI says, the 'synthesis of his precepts'[10], the word that sums up all his divine desires[11], the 'peak of the Gospel'[12], and since the abandonment, the means to accomplishing unity, is the climax of the suffering which Christ offered for our salvation, it is clear that every other expression of his doctrine or of his life can be found, in a certain way, in unity and in the abandonment. Indeed, it will logically find its full meaning in the Testament of Jesus and in the peak of his suffering.

This explains why numerous religious priests who have been in contact with the Movement from its birth, discovered that there was certainly nothing that could disturb their own spirituality. On the contrary, they discovered a light that enkindled their own spirituality and helped them to understand it better. They felt that the two things were perfectly compatible. The spirituality of unity helps to develop the potentialities already inherent in one's own vocation and, at the same time, enriches it with new values.

The effects produced in those who participate in the charism of unity are very consoling. More than fourteen thousand religious priests of 124 institutes and about forty-four thousand women religious are in contact with the spirituality and the life of the Movement.

Through the light of this charism of our time, they affirm, for instance, that they understand their founder better. A new love is born for him; at times, an appreciation that they were not aware of before and a strong desire to re-live and to actualize his charism in the Church today. Moreover, in getting to know their founder more deeply, they affirm that they rediscover their rule and that they feel a greater desire to put it into practice.

In addition, having understood more about their founder leads them to a profound unity with the superiors who represent him. In the common father or mother, they recognize that they are children of the same religious family. All this favours the presence of Jesus in the midst of a community united in this way. He enlightens and gives value to all its aspects. He gives meaning to all its expressions.

Thus we witness a real and true renewal of the community, with an increase in vocations, and new developments in the missions. Superiors have the possibility of entrusting difficult tasks to persons they can truly depend on.

Moreover, we can see a real and profound communion among the members of the different orders, making possible the sense of ecclesial unity; likewise, between religious and secular priests, and between religious priests and dedicated lay people. This leads to each one feeling a living part not only of a religious family, but of the Church. This leads also to the renewal of the Church.

The contribution of the religious to the Movement

Dear priests and brothers, before concluding this talk regarding the spirituality of the Focolare Movement and the religious, I would like to answer a question that might come up. If this is the contribution of the Movement to the religious, what is the contribution of the religious to the Movement?

All the members of the Movement have always drunk from the holy founders. Who deepened our understanding of prayer if not Teresa of Avila? Who underlined our poverty more clearly, if not Saint Francis? Who gave a deeper meaning to our small Christian towns, if not Saint Benedict? Who increased our love towards everyone, especially towards the most needy and those who suffer the most, if not Saint Vincent de Paul and Saint Camillus de Lellis?

Yes, throughout these years the saints have always accompanied us and helped us greatly. They have confirmed our charism with their own.

Hence, there is an exchange of gifts between the Focolare Movement and the world of religious, as is required by the fact that we are all members of one another in the Mystical Body of Christ (cf. 1 Cor. 12:4–27).

Perhaps it is also for this reason – and we cannot deny this – that much good has been given to the Church by the Movement. As we have often been told, it is certainly not the work of human beings, but of God.

REFERENCES

1 G.B. Montini, *Discorsi dell'Arcivescovo di Milano 'Su la Madonna e su i santi'* 1955–1962, Milan 1965, p.461.

2 Ibid.

3 cf. John Paul II, *Talk* to the Focolare Movement, Mariapolis Centre, Rocca di Papa, August 19, 1984, in the *Osservatore Romano* (Italian edition) of August 20–21, 1984, p.5.

4 Focolarine is the Italian plural of the name for people who live in a focolare house.

5 'Mariapolis' means city of Mary.

6 cf. Thérèse of Lisieux, *Lettere*, n. 127, in *Gli scritti*, Rome, 1970, p. 597.

7 i.e., John 17.

8 cf. Paul VI, *L'azione dello Spirito Santo nel Corpo mistico di Cristo*, Rome, November 24, 1971, in *Insegnamenti di Paolo VI*, IX, op. cit. p. 1072.

9 Paul VI, *Inserirsi nella circolazione universale della carità del Signore*, March 30, 1972, in *Insegnamenti di Paolo VI*, X, 1973, p. 322.

10 Paul VI, *La via maestra verso l'ecumenismo*, January 21, 1973, in *Insegnamenti di Paolo VI*, XI, 1974, p. 56.

11 cf. Paul VI, *Homily* at the close of the week of prayer for unity of Christians, Rome, January 25, 1973, in *Insegnamenti di Paolo VI*, XI, Ibid. 1974, p. 84.

12 Paul VI, *Lavorare con fervore affinché le varie istituzioni siano animate da autentico spirito cristiano*, June 8, 1974, in *Insegnamenti di Paolo VI*, 1975, p. 532.

APPENDIX

The Spirituality of Unity and the Renewal of Religious Life

T. Bissett OMI

We are all aware of the crisis that has affected religious life, and the whole Church, in the last twenty years. A quick glance at the literature shows up words and headings, such as 'chaos', 'confusion', 'transition', 'renewal', that leave us without any illusions as to the state of religious life today. It is in sharp contrast to the period leading up to the Second Vatican Council, when everything seemed to be thriving: numbers were continually increasing, the organic structures were stable, expectations and practice were consistent and universal, and everything was clear-cut.

When all seemed secure, religious were suddenly confronted with an unexpected task: to modify, remodel, renew. This was to 'comprise both a constant return to the sources of the whole of the Christian life and to the primitive inspiration of the institutes, and their adaption to the changed conditions of our time' (PC 2). Great confusion and uncertainty ensued, and large numbers left the religious life. Among those who remained, many took the call to renewal seriously, while others coped by a variety of imbalanced stances such as fundamentalism or extreme liberalism. The 70's were the most turbulant years, when many of the familiar structures and symbols were disregarded or diminished, and nothing had taken their place. It was something of a culture-shock, and indeed coincided with a world that was in deep turmoil, where the process of secularization was in full motion. People felt stunned, rootless, and very insecure. The acceptance and prestige that priests and religious had been accustomed to were becoming undermined.

Gerald Arbuckle, one of the most influential writers on the topic at this time, identified four types of escape from this new culturally-disagreeable environment:

1. Withdrawal from religious life.

2. "Reverse Nativism": going back to the symbols of predictability and certainty of the former Catholic sub-culture. (The Lefebvre Movement is an example of this).

3. Cultural Romanticism: believing that the new culture now facing us is *the* culture, disregarding the past and taking on in an uncritical way new values that crumble after the initial enthusiasm.

4. 'Cargo Cultism': destroying old structures and replacing them with new ones. (Once Chapters of renewal had been held, new Rules and Constitutions written, new structures of government introduced, then many religious expected that by sitting and waiting, the renewal would take place automatically.)[1]

These are all ways of escaping a crisis, but a true response involves more than a few minor adjustments; it calls for a radical conversion to the Lord in the light of the new situation. The eighties have been years of facing up to the question realistically. The time of shock has given way to the realization that this change is here to stay, that we are never going to return to the way things were before. The increase in vocations in Ireland in 1980, thought by many to be the beginning or return of an upward pattern, has proved to be only a temporary reprieve before a definite downward direction that has persisted right through the decade,[2] a pattern that is in keeping with most other counties in Europe and North America. Many worried religious keep asking: 'why are they not coming to us?' It is easy to settle for answers such as the young people's inability to make permanent commitments today; there is some element of truth in this, but it could blind us to the obvious truth that they are not attracted to a style of religious life that is still prevalent, and unless renewal takes place there will be no future. This realization is being taken seriously by many, as evidenced by the elaborate processes of renewal undertaken by many congregations, and by the number of renewal courses and seminars on offer. The implications of this have been keenly felt by those involved in formation. At the Congress on Formation organized by the Religious Movement of the Focolare in Rome, January, 1988, Fr. Callisto Vendrame, Superior General of the Camillians, based his talk on the question: 'What kind of formation, and for what kind of Religious Life?' He says that 'formation depends on the concept one has of religious life and how one lives it, on the image which one forms and projects of the religious.'³ Formators find themselves in the uncomfortable position of trying to form people according to a style that seems to be called for, but which is not easily found in practice. The transition from formation communities into established communities is often very difficult, and leaves one with the question whether it is possible or advisable to put the new wine into old wineskins.

All this would seem to present a very gloomy picture, but that depends on the meaning we give the facts. History indicates that there are life cycles through which every religious congregation passes, and each cycle comprises certain distinct phases. First of all there is the foundation period, followed by a lengthy expansion period in which the foundation charism is institutionalized in a variety of ways. This may last two or three generations before the stabilization period comes in. Eventually the seeming immutability of this period begins to give way after fifty or a hundred years, and the community enters the breakdown period where stress and doubt accompany the dismantling of the structures and belief systems that had served so well for so long. Finally there comes the critical period in which three outcomes are possible: extinction, minimal survival, or revitalization.⁴

Historically, 64% of all men's religious orders founded before 1800 became extinct, and only 11% have a current membership of over 2000. Three characteristics can be singled out in the communities that have been revitalized: a transforming response to the signs of the times, a reappropriation of the founding charism, and a profound renewal of the life of prayer, faith, and centredness in Christ. Personal conversion is central in this, and the community experiences the revitalization as a second foundation.[5]

Apart from the pattern of any individual congregation, similar cycles seem to exist in the general history of religious life. The major eras were the desert Fathers, then monasticism, the mendicant orders, the apostolic orders, and finally the largely teaching orders of the nineteenth century. The Second Vatican Council marked the beginning of the breakdown period of the era that began around 1800, and we are now coming to the critical stage where new questions are being seriously asked, and where choices must be made that will determine either extinction or a future for religious orders. So it is a time of hope for those interested in a future, it is a time to let go what hinders, and to choose what is life-giving. Just as an individual must pass through a process of grieving when facing death or bereavement, so must religious life as we have known it up to now: after going through the various stages of denial, anger, bargaining, and depression, we are now faced with the call to a willing acceptance of a passover journey.

In each of the major eras, there has been a shift in the dominant image of religious life, and these shifts seemed to occur when there were major shifts in society as well as the Church at large. The signs are clear that we are ready for another major shift, that the form which served so well for so long must now give way to something new. Where does this new form come from? How can we identify it? Again historically it would seem that each major shift in the dominant image of religious life is heralded by some significantly new foundations which embody a new image in an especially striking way. Examples of this in the past have been the Benedictines, the Franciscans, the Jesuits. In an historical analysis, Diarmuid O Murchú includes the Focolare among a few movements or congregations that he considers to be the pioneers of a new quality of religious life, which may become the norm for the next century. He adds that 'foundresses like Mother Teresa and Chiara Lubich are women of great spiritual integrity, and their contribution to the future of religious life is widely acknowledged and appreciated.'[6] It is not necessarily the structures that such new institutes establish for themselves that matter, but rather the new spirit and insights that bring fresh light on living the Gospel in a new age.

The spirituality of the Focolare Movement is essentially one of unity, and has shown through experience not only how the Gospel can be lived in a fresh and radical way, but also how it throws new light on existing charisms and unites them in a particular way. It is a revitalizing force at this critical time, offering hope and direction, embodying at the same time the values of fidelity to the Church and particular congregation, and facing the new situation of the modern age. At a time when religious life is attracting fewer people, this life of unity attracts people of every age-group, but particularly the young.

From the early days of the Movement, religious have come into contact and discovered that, rather than drawing them away from their own congregations, it brought light and freshness that enabled them to rediscover and live their own charism with a new vision. At the Congress in Rome, Chiara Lubich explained how 'the spirituality of unity helps to develop the potentialities already inherent in one's own vocation and, at the same time, enriches it with new values.'[7] Many religious found that the charism of unity helped them to understand their founders and foundresses better, even well before the Vatican Council called on them to move in that direction. It brought a fresh way of living the Gospel, and helped religious to see that each charism incarnated a certain passage of scripture which gave a particular tone to the whole Gospel. It threw light on ways of reaching out to different generations in a fast-changing world, especially the young generation; for this it utilized all the means of communication at its disposal, such as music, mime, audio-visuals, and so on. It used the fruits of modern technology in order to reach people and communicate its experience.

An item on the agenda of nearly every Chapter and Congress in the last twenty years has been that of community life, and especially in the context of the search for an appropriate spirituality for apostolic communities. It is clear that religious communities had for so long been operating from a strong monastic and institutional basis. In practice there was very little to distinguish the novitiate of a monastic order from that of an apostolic or missionary congregation. To change a mentality that has existed for hundreds of years is a very major task; people must learn to dialogue, to listen to one another's expectations and fears, to let go of fixed positions, and to discern new directions. The spirituality of unity emphasizes listening to one another in a non-judgmental way, because it is only when a person is loved and accepted as he or she is that there is the freedom to give to others. This is motivated by the Gospel saying of Jesus, 'whatever you do to the least of these, you do to me' (Matt. 25:40). You make yourself one with your neighbour by being empty before him or her, and by so doing you are loving Christ. We are called to live this first of all among ourselves, and then with the people we are called to minister to. This is not the false kind of kenosis that has often been promoted in the past; to be really empty before another requires a great level of wholeness and maturity, of awareness and freedom, of openness and love.

When this quality of relating is reciprocated, when each is prepared to give his or her life for the other, then there is the reality of Jesus in the midst. In the life of the Focolare, it is this presence which replaces the monastic walls and structures, and it is only made possible when people are living the new commandment of mutual love. This has great significance for religious who are coming out of an age of great individualism. The word 'community' has been thrown around so much in recent years that it can mean anything from the deepest intimacy to external structures, and it can lose the essence of what the Lord intended for his disciples. 'Communion' or 'communitas' might capture something closer to its deepest meaning. It is not about programmes or systems; it is not about feeling comfortable with each other; it is not about living together for some project. It is rather about people living for each other.[8] Talking about apostolic community, John Futrell says that 'community exists when these persons experience themselves striving together to realize their communion.'[9] It is the bonding that takes place between disciples who are committed to loving each other as Christ loved them. This communion is not something that can be sought for in itself, but is the reality of a community on mission. When this bonding is experienced, then there is no longer fear of letting go familiar structures or heading into unknown territories, because there is a new quality of life that makes all things possible.

Here we can also see how community life becomes integrated into mission, giving a basis for an understanding of apostolic spirituality. If Christ is present in the community, he is not there in a passive way. His life is one of mission, and such a community co-operates with him in his mission. Christ unified all the different aspects in his life: being with his disciples, going off alone to pray, reaching out to people with his message of salvation, rejoicing and weeping with whoever he met. The dichotomy between contemplation and action only emerged in history, and we are having difficulty finding an integrated approach. This is where the experience of the Focolare Movement of having Jesus in the midst can help us change from the image of monks on mission to a more integrated spirituality.

The communion and unity that one can experience in this way is made possible to the extent that each individual unites himself with the crucified Lord. The cry of Jesus on the cross, 'My God, my God, why have you forsaken me?' has a central place in the spirituality of unity. Jesus Forsaken is the key to unity with God and with the neighbour. He can become the real model for religious who feel confused, dejected, isolated, afraid, uncertain, divided, irrelevant. While psychology and sociology have made a great contribution to our growing understanding of the individual and the group, they do not in themselves have any transforming power. It is the Spirit within us who brings about change within us and in the world around us. By embracing Jesus Forsaken in the sufferings that we experience, in all the hurts, the fears, the doubts, the anxieties, his work of redemption is taking place in us and in the world around us.

Another particular point of interest for many congregations is that of Mary. She, who has a place in the title or spirituality of nearly every Religious Congregation, is being discovered in a new light as someone with much more than mere devotional significance. The spirituality of unity has thrown fresh light on the place of Mary in our lives and in the Church. She is perceived as someone close to us, to whom we can relate. As the first disciple, she is a model for all of us in our spiritual journey. By offering herself as a creature, and giving her "yes", she enabled the Word to become incarnate. Her role was in the background, to be a blank page on which God's Word could be written, the silence in which the Word could speak. In her words, 'behold the handmaid of the Lord', she declares herself nothing in the sight of God, and he fills her with himself to such an extent that the Word takes flesh in her. One of the first members of the Movement points out the significance of this for our lives: 'Beneath every word of Jesus there was the presence of Mary, and the words of Jesus were always supported by Mary's silence. And we discovered that if we live the words of Jesus, the Word of Life, we are putting ourselves at the service of God as Mary did, and if we seek to live Christ again, we find that in fact we are living Mary who bore her Creator in herself and gave him to the world.'[10] So as apostolic religious we are called to give birth to Jesus in ourselves and in our communities, so that we can give him to the world. In this way we are living Mary with the focus on Christ, an emphasis that the Church has been clearly giving since the Vatican Council.[11]

A final dimension that is new and most exciting is the communion of charisms which is made possible through the spirituality of unity. The founders were men and women who did not live for themselves, but whose experience of love and service made them universal-minded, disposed for the fulfilment of Christ's last testament, 'that all may be one.' For a long time there had been the tendency for each congregation to think mainly of themselves and their own life and mission, with very little contact between the different groups. That has changed considerably, and we see ample evidence of sharing and collaboration at many levels. The spirituality of unity enables them to take a step beyond mere collaboration, and to have the reality of Jesus in their midst. This unity of charisms is a particularly rich experience of Church. Tertullian once pointed out that 'where three are gathered together, even if they are laymen, there is the Church.'[12] An extension of that idea could be made in our context today: where three religious, even if they are from different congregations, are gathered together in my name, there is the Church. If religious are to be prophetic voices in a Church that is striving for unity at all levels, then their unity among themselves is a powerful witness to, and at the same time a foretaste of the 'ut omnes', that unity Christ prayed for before he died.

REFERENCES
1. cf. Gerald A. Arbuckle, *Strategies for Growth in Religious Life*, St Paul Publications, Slough, 1986, pp. 16ff.
2. cf. *Vocations in Ireland 1988*, published by the Council for Research and Development, Maynooth.
3. This is awaiting publication.
4. cf. Cada et al, *Shaping the Coming Age of Religious Life*, Affirmation Books, Whitinsville, Massachusetts, 1979, pp. 51ff.
5. Ibid., pp.59ff.
6. Diarmuid O Murchú, *The Seed Must Die*, Veritas, Dublin, 1980.
7. See above p. 213
8. cf. Eamonn Bredin, *Disturbing the Peace: the Way of Disciples*, Twenty Third Publications, Mystic, Connecticut, 1986, p. 134.
9. John C. Futrell, Evaluating Apostolic Communities, in *Human Development*. Summer, 1986.
10. *Gen Re*, English ed., April 1988, p.3.
11. cf. especially *Marialis Cultus*, no. 25.
12. Quoted in Chiara Lubich, *Where Two or Three*, New City, London, 1977, p. 16.